An IT Tale

A Program Manager's Journey

EMC Consulting

First published by Dog Ear Publishing
4010 W. 86th Street, Ste H
Indianapolis, IN 46268
www.dogearpublishing.net

ISBN: 978-160844-359-8

This book is printed on acid-free paper.

Printed in the United States of America

FOREWORD

An IT Tale – A Program Manager's Journey provides insight into the realities of the corporate IT world. It offers useful examples for running an IT organization as a business and delivering real value to the entire organization. It also examines human issues that are central to successful technology implementations as it follows the ups and downs of managing investments of time, energy, morale, and millions of dollars. This book reminds us that amidst technical complexity it remains necessary to focus on the relationships among people, processes, and systems. It brings to life the IT adventure as it presents the reality of delivering an IT product while navigating a major corporation's political pitfalls.

CHAPTER 1

Charles Henry Dowd pressed the call button on the elevator bank for floors 34 through 42. He awaited the next car that would take him up to the executive level where the Board of Directors would soon convene. Tugging a bit harder at his tie than he meant to, he realized it felt especially tight around his throat. He could feel his carotid artery pulsing against his collar as he wiped away small beads of perspiration from his upper lip. Any casual observer would see a well dressed man in his fifties, with a neatly trimmed but thinning mane of salt and pepper hair waiting calmly by the elevator door, a leather portfolio in his left hand, a simple gold wedding band, and a weighty Naval Academy ring on his right hand.

But Charlie, as he was known to friends and colleagues alike, was not as calm as he appeared. He knew the next hour would dictate whether his reputation for success would grow, or he would be forced into early retirement. After more than a year of late nights, hard won victories, near critical errors and alliances forged, lost, and forged again, he wasn't certain.

Roughly sixteen months earlier, Charlie had assumed the role of Chief Information Officer for Unidigitel. Unidigitel, a Fortune 100 multi-service communications operator, was born largely from the mergers of a former Bell Operating Company and several aggressive competitive communications providers. He had left a lucrative post with a major financial institution where for nearly five years he'd been CIO. He'd led his company through a massive IT and product definition overhaul that allowed it to regain its once envied positions in the portfolio management, high net-worth clientele, credit card and equity trading sectors while its chief competitors were weighed down by risky mortgage bets and poor management. Charlie had stepped down just before Christmas to take a long anticipated break. He spent time with his wife, his daughter's family and his three grandchildren. But he had earned significant cachet as a transformation expert, and his reputation ultimately brought Unidigitel to his doorstep five months later.

The communications giant made him a financial offer that he could not refuse. He felt he was too young to retire and fancied the idea of leaving the smothering pressures of New York's tumultuous Wall Street in order to head back to the West Coast where his brothers and their families still lived. Unidigitel also presented a series of intriguing challenges. It was in the unfortunate position of losing money, customers and competitive advantage to more nimble nemeses. These competitors were dealing better with post-merger challenges and had begun to adopt technologies that allowed them to bring new, advanced services to market.

Unidigitel, on the other hand, had already invested a year in its IT transformation program and had dismissed its previous CIO, Bradley Forrester. The purpose of the transformation had been to simplify operations; achieve customer-centricity through common, web-based customer interaction tools for its call centers, retail stores, and online portals; and to deliver bundled voice, video, wireless and Internet services that allowed customers to access content and use applications across them all. It was an ambitious undertaking, but necessary to regain Unidigitel's once coveted market leadership position. Forrester had proven unable to align the IT organization with Unidigitel's business organizations and had managed the transformation program incompetently.

A first time executive with a background in software development, Forrester held an undergraduate degree in computer science from Cornell and a graduate degree in electrical engineering from MIT. He was intelligent, but too focused on technology to be an effective business leader. He was also arrogant and had little patience for those who could not instantly understand his rapid and rambling techno-speak.

Within the span of a year, Forrester had lost the respect and loyalty of his team and his peers. He had degraded morale within the IT organization by demanding his people work late nights and weekend hours without overtime or bonus incentives. He shielded himself in his technical world, dictated to business owners rather than engaging them, and overlooked simple solutions in lieu of what he considered advanced approaches that proved to be overly complicated. As things began to go wrong, Forrester restricted his staff's communication with other departments and blamed others publicly for his failures. When this led to conflicts with various business owners who were impacted by his decisions, he failed to go to bat for the project managers who ended up in the direct line of fire.

After just 10 months as CIO for Unidigitel, Forrester's glorious transformation program was nothing more than a bloated, big systems play that had missed its key targets; was $30 million over budget; and had been rated by several major news and tech magazines as the biggest IT boondoggle of the year. The Chairman of the Board did not bother to scold or berate Brad when the decision was made to let him go. He simply told CEO Liz Fagan to "replace that idiot with someone useful." He made it clear to her that she had best find a CIO who could set things on the correct path within a year, or she'd follow Brad out the door. Forrester's dismissal came in late April with little ceremony as security escorted him quietly from the campus and movers arrived after business hours to clear out his office.

Liz Fagan, a dynamic personality and media darling, had been CEO of Unidigitel for nearly a year and half when Forrester was hired to lead her IT group. Forrester had not been her first choice for the post, but when her top candidate decided to take a senior position with a major pharmaceutical company, and her second candidate was diagnosed with a debilitating illness, Forrester was forced upon her as the favorite son of one of Unidigitel's senior Board members and major shareholders.

When the company's stock price weakened and traders began to short the company aggressively, that particular Board member divested himself of his shares, surrendered his board seat, and ran for the exit. Fagan was left with an unmitigated disaster on her hands and a CIO with whom she could not communicate effectively. When she recommended Forrester's dismissal to the Chairman, he replied, "you can sacrifice a man and seal the hatch, but you still need to save the ship. Get it done."

Though the Chairman readily voiced his displeasure, he would not deflect blame entirely for Forrester's hiring and could not deny Fagan's value. Her positive relationship with the media was an asset. She was quick on her feet and deeply intelligent. She earned loyalty quickly among her peers and subordinates with a casual confidence and competitive spirit born of her days as a college athlete. Though the company was ailing in the public eye, Fagan was rarely disparaged in the media. She was honest about the company's need for change and the tangible challenges involved in overhauling a massive but aging organization.

Fagan knew, however, that smiles and clever turns of phrase would only get her so far. Restoring the market's and her customers' confidence in the company was the bottom line, and she knew if she failed to do it, she'd might not be given another chance at a CEO position again. She saw what had happened to other high profile, female executives in technology companies and did not want her burgeoning career and positive reputation to suffer the same fate. She knew she needed real help, real fast, and she knew that Charlie Dowd was the person she needed to keep her company – and her career – from crashing into the proverbial mountain.

Charlie, nearly 15 years Fagan's senior, had been a mentor to Liz earlier in her career. She had graduated from Georgia Tech where, in addition to being a track athlete, she earned dual degrees in mechanical engineering and computer science. She went to work for a major aircraft avionics manufacturer and quickly moved through the ranks to become a project manager and then product manager in just a few years. In her first week with the company, she made an appointment to meet with the Senior Vice President of Product Development, one Charlie Dowd. She quickly impressed him with her knowledge of the company, its competitive position in the market and the potential for its various product lines.

Dowd kept an eye on Fagan during the next year, occasionally calling her to see how she was faring and making sure she was at the top of the list for any appropriate promotions that came along. He never told her about his behind-the-scenes influence on her career. On an oversold, cross-country flight to a trade exhibition, Fagan was upgraded to first class, into the empty seat next to Charlie's.

He had wanted to get some sleep, but she was bursting at the seams with energy about an idea she'd had while driving home from work a few days earlier. He listened begrudgingly at first, but soon realized that she was on to something big. Her idea for creating a personal version of the company's digital aircraft navigation system would prove to be brilliant, opening new markets in consumer electronics and automotive accessories that management had not ever considered before.

Charlie Dowd was at Yankee Stadium, enjoying his son-in-law's box seats, on a cool day for baseball in late April when he spied an email from Liz Fagan on his Blackberry. After the game he called her back. She told him of the problems she was having. After several follow up conversations in the next couple of weeks, and with the right incentives in place, Charlie decided to go back to work. He'd put his own reputation on the line to help his most successful protégé who had been so helpful to him.

Charlie believed when he agreed to join the company that walking into what appeared to be a sinking ship could actually be a great opportunity. Unidigitel had a well known brand and massive distribution channels. It had deep pockets and talented people that just needed to be set back on a successful path. From the outside looking in, and given his success at his previous post, he was confident that he could help the company recover and grow.

Nearly seventeen months later, as another Labor Day rolled by, Charlie was certain he'd done his best for his friend, but he still wasn't sure the Chairman would be satisfied with his results. As he waited for the elevator, he pinpointed that it was six months in when he'd begun to suspect subconsciously that things were even worse than he'd initially estimated. As problems with poor data, inevitable development delays, and budget constraints mounted roughly nine months in, he realized his initial estimates had been a bit too optimistic. He knew the board of directors didn't have the stomach for much of a margin of error. As he prepared for this meeting, he had to hope the early returns the program was showing would be enough to sate the board and maintain their support for the program and his tenure as CIO.

He knew he'd get some credit for climbing out of the hole his predecessor had dug. He knew he'd shown the Board that the hole went even deeper than its members had imagined when he'd given them a "state of the union" review after his first 60 days as CIO. But he questioned whether he could convince them that he was *only* two months behind where he'd planned to be after spending tens of millions of additional dollars and setting lofty – perhaps too lofty – expectations for sales and organizational improvements. He knew the benefits he'd promised were just around the corner. He wondered if the Board would consider his promises empty ones and perceive his effort as just another nearsighted boondoggle forced on them by a bit-head who was merely less incompetent than Forrester had been.

He'd started out on this path to help Liz Fagan out of a tight spot that could derail her career. Today, it was his reputation and legacy that concerned him. As the digital ring sounded to signal that the elevator he'd been waiting for had reached the first floor he took a deep breath, stepped through the open doors, and pressed the button for the 42nd floor.

As he'd waded into the fray in his first couple of weeks with Unidigitel, Charlie realized that the company's problems went much deeper than an inexperienced CIO and poor IT business alignment. Unidigitel was bleeding cash as a result of poor billing and revenue management processes that were wrapped around more than a dozen disparate billing systems. These were the result of years of product-specific management and the legacy of acquired entities that were never really integrated into the fold.

For years IT wasn't viewed as a strategic asset. A simplistic and disjointed approach led various business owners to launch their own IT projects out of frustration. They had become accustomed to an inefficient, "go it alone" approach. Charlie saw several shadow organizations embedded in the company that he would have to consolidate. These were IT groups that had been formed tactically within different business organizations. They operated independently and weren't governed under any common structure. This had been the case in his previous post as well, but the resistance to change he would find among business units that Forrester had disenfranchised was far more intense.

Most of the business leaders he'd met with during his first month simply didn't believe that a new CIO would be any more effective than Forrester had been. Groups within the company's billing, care, telephony, wireless, and video divisions had become so fatigued by Forrester's dictatorial approach that initially they weren't willing to make cooperating with Charlie any kind of a priority. Forrester had never taken the time to solicit their opinions or understand their needs. When Charlie came to call on them, they were automatically suspicious of his actual motives.

On a macro level, communication between the various divisions was extremely poor. This resulted in products that were managed and supported separately on an increasing basis. Customers were confused about those products, how they were priced, and where to call for support when things went wrong. The customer experience was disjointed. Simple problems that should have been resolved easily with access to the right information were not. Opportunities for positive customer interactions turned into losses. Customers and care agents struggled to navigate their ways through Unidigitel's morass of call centers, interactive voice response systems, care applications, and online support sites that looked and behaved differently while providing conflicting information.

When Forrester began enforcing his changes, he failed to address these organizational problems first. Instead he exacerbated them by applying a technology-centric approach. He believed these business problems were merely the result of a disorganized and aging systems infrastructure. His plan was to migrate all of the critical customer-facing systems like billing, CRM, product management, and all customer and product data to a new and extremely complex architecture. Fundamentally he was correct. The existing systems infrastructure wouldn't support business improvements or customer-centricity goals.

His approach, however, was fatally flawed. He took on a "best of breed" strategy that involved nearly a dozen new IT vendors. He fell in love with buzz words like "web services," but didn't evaluate whether these were aligned with the overall business goals of his transformation program. Worst of all, he failed to engage business owners and user groups early on to determine whether his architectural vision was even feasible.

Figuring the organization would embrace new technologies whole heartedly, Forrester took a clean-slate approach to his new architecture. This generated extreme resistance to change. It also failed to leverage the experienced people in different business units who knew how the company ran day to day and had the insight needed to redesign and prioritize the process improvements that needed to be made.

When Forrester began announcing his planned changes to people across the company, he was stunned by the resistance he'd faced. Rather than recognizing that he'd created it by failing to include affected stakeholders in the planning stages, he reacted belligerently. He assumed no one was smart enough to understand what he was trying to do. He decided to push forward stubbornly with an "I'll show them" attitude. He retreated deeper into his shell and communicated even less than he had previously.

When he began pulling his technology vendors into his labs and it dawned on him and them that his architecture plan might be too elaborate, too convoluted, and counted too much on unproven components, it was too late to change direction without losing face. He blamed vendors. He blamed project managers. He'd even misstated some of his budget updates to the CFO to hide the depth of his errors. When Fagan dismissed him and security came to see him off, he strutted down the nearly empty halls like Caligula. In his own mind he remained convinced that he'd done nothing wrong and that he was tragically misunderstood.

Charlie didn't particularly care about what Forrester thought of himself. He'd seen rookies make these mistakes before. What concerned him, as he began talking to other executives and digging through audit reports, were the aftereffects of Forrester's misdeeds. Headhunters attacked the company like sharks in a feeding frenzy. Some of Unidigitel's best sales people and account managers had already jumped ship for other operators and started cherry picking their best accounts. Good project and operations managers – people with critical knowledge about how the company functioned – were either gone or were looking to leave.

As Charlie read through a pile of audit reports that had been dropped off at his office before he'd even moved in, he could see that the auditors were struggling to get straight answers out of Forrester's chief lieutenants who knew they'd soon follow their old boss out into the street. He recognized very quickly that he had more to learn about Unidigitel's inner workings, and more to fix, than he'd anticipated. He'd have to spend significant time winning key allies in groups like the CFO's organization, in sales, marketing and customer care. Not only would he have to plug the deep holes Forrester had created, he'd have to be a change agent for the company's culture.

Charlie came from a completely different school of thought from Forrester. His military experience gave him a sense of accountability and responsibility. He knew what it meant to solve big problems with limited resources at hand, and that bad news never improves with age. He also believed that sometimes he needed to ask himself whether it was him or the rest of the world that's crazy. Typically, the answer was not the rest of the world. This ability to be self-critical, to admit mistakes in order to fix them and to turn those mistakes into opportunities for success were key personality traits. They had made Charlie a successful leader and consensus builder throughout his career. His philosophies aside, however, there just wasn't much time to turn things around. He knew that IT transformations were always akin to changing the tires on a truck while it was screaming down a highway. He quoted this truism often. In this case, however, Unidigitel was more like a train than a truck given the scope of its IT base, the breadth of its operations, and the depth of its organizational issues.

These problems were compounded by increasing competition from traditional rivals. They were pushing multi-service product bundles into Unidigitel's residential markets. Meeting, or better, beating these competitors would require vastly improved technical capabilities to be introduced in the face of extreme price competition. What had been healthy margins on traditional services like telephony were squeezed down to tiny fractions. Unidigitel needed to introduce new, more innovative, and better integrated products to market faster with simpler billing. The company also needed better customer education and support, which wouldn't be possible with Unidigitel's disparate, silo-oriented sales, product support and care organizations. Massive changes were unavoidable.

In Charlie's opinion, the CIO's job as a change agent was to use IT to help implement business improvements for the sake of the business, not simply for the sake of adopting new technologies. He knew from experience that business owners usually didn't like to change. They often believed their success was predicated on their tried-and-true methodologies, especially when they were accustomed to operating independently. And he could see that Forrester had only made it more difficult for him to convince the business owners that, with all due respect to their past success, aligning their efforts would result in even greater and more sustainable gains for everyone.

Charlie's first six weeks were intense. As a "get your hands dirty" type of manager, he attended various business owners' regular staff meetings. Fagan, as CEO, had empowered him to do this, but he wanted to approach this tender situation somewhat gingerly at first. He began as a purely neutral observer, sitting quietly on the sidelines and listening, only providing comments or perspectives when asked to do so. He realized that this was the only way to figure out "how stuff works" because, after all, it was his job to explain to other C-level executives and the board how "stuff was working" and how it needed to change.

He needed to understand everything from how up-sales were conducted to how orders for new cell phones were processed. He needed to know what it took to process bills, apply discounts, and perform collections. He needed a complete understanding of how support centers – both on and off-shore – fielded, routed, handled and resolved calls from customers; what information different contact center agents could access; and how the centers interacted with each other. He would then need to gauge what tools business owners wish they had, which processes they felt were the most limiting, and what kinds of changes they'd embrace and believed should be prioritized. Ultimately he'd have to explain to them what was feasible within the context of the transformation program. He'd have to find ways to satisfy them with a healthy dose of give and take.

In order to get to know the key individuals in charge of various business units and groups within them, he would invite them to lunch or dinner and encourage them to vent about Forrester and other frustrations they'd had with their IT systems. Some were more forthcoming than others. Not everyone accepted his invitations readily. But his aim was to try to build trust by listening, empathizing, and demonstrating that he understood that poor IT systems and processes were affecting their business responsibilities. He also made it a personal priority to spend time with the troops by having lunch with them in the cafeteria and walking the halls, joining casual conversations, and insisting they call him "Charlie" and never "Mr. Dowd."

Dropping in on one such conversation during his very first week on Unidigitel's campus, he overheard a group of young analysts and developers complaining that Mr. Dowd, the new CIO – who they did not yet recognize in person – was probably just some new stuffed shirt who would be no better than Forrester. He joined the conversation, introduced himself as a new manager named Charlie, and agreed that most of the time these executive changes just replaced one clod with another.

He shared an anecdote about a previous job he'd had with a telecom company where a CEO change had taken place and one stuffed shirt who failed to meet the streets expectations was for some reason replaced with a near clone. The two men looked a little bit alike, used the same corporate-speak in their presentations, and had been recruited away from similar positions in the same major telecom company. They had such similar wardrobes that employees began to joke that they actually had the same mother who dressed them every morning.

The group chuckled at this as one young developer who actually worked for one Unidigitel's software vendors asked him, "What did you say your name was again?" Charlie shook the young man's hand, smiled and said deadpan, "I'm Charles Dowd – the new clone." The five young employees stood stiff, in shock, their careers flashing before their eyes, until Charlie said, "Don't worry guys. I'm with you. If you ever want to come into my office and complain about the new stuffed shirt, my door is always open."

It was this kind of casual interaction that would help to foster loyalty from the bottom up, though Charlie knew he was walking a fine line between earning trust and being a pal. He knew that when it came time to drop the hammer, it was his hammer to drop. But refreshing in the minds of folks at all levels of the organization that they each had important roles to play – and that they would be rewarded for performance - was critical to driving a positive cultural change for the entire business.

Earning the trust of peers at the top of the organization was an equally important and even greater challenge for Charlie. The CFO, Langdon Willis III, was a tough old battleaxe. He was a CPA with an investment banking background who scrutinized numbers, budgets and ROI measurements with uncommon impunity. He was recognized publicly as someone who instituted strong controls, was an advocate for tight financial management, but was no bean counter. He understood how to invest dollars in the business and was considered to have a well-balanced approach.

At the point Charlie joined Unidigitel, Willis was just plain angry. Forrester had lied to him about his expenses and budgets and never invited him, or any liaison from his organization, into his secretive, closed-door meetings. This put all of Unidigitel, and Willis and Fagan in particular, in a dangerous and risky situation, particularly in light of Sarbanes-Oxley requirements. Charlie eased his trepidation a bit in his first few weeks by appealing to his need for control by asking him specifically to consider adding a finance liaison to the program management team he was building.

He acknowledged Forrester's failure to "keep the books clean" and laid out his approach based on cooperation, full disclosure of the project, its costs, its value and its returns. Charlie wanted "Lang," as the other executives called him, to understand that as an IT leader, he had no desire to be a lawyer or a CPA. He wanted get the work done and utilize the best experts from outside of the IT organization to support that work.

Charlie expressed to Willis that he had no desire to bring in his own people to create a shadow finance organization within IT. He noted that in addition to an attaché from finance, he'd engage with the supply chain organization to enforce controls around procurement contracts; tie supplier's contracts, payments and bonuses to performance milestones; and would try to fix some of the bad contracts Forrester had allowed to be signed.

Willis played his cards close to the vest at first, listening to Charlie with a stern expression, though occasionally nodding his head in assent. At the end of Charlie's first pitch to him, Willis looked him straight in the eye and said, "This all sounds good on paper, but I'll believe it when I see it. That said, if you're serious about your offer, I think Michael Kim from my staff is probably the guy for you."

"Fair enough," Charlie thought to himself as he shook Willis's hand. He decidedly immediately that he respected Willis for his matter-of-fact approach and had confidence that over time, he could earn his trust through frank discourse and well measured and financially justified actions.

Earning the Chairman of the Board's trust and respect was also critical and not easily accomplished. Roger Schultz was a highly respected individual who had made his mark in the 1980s as a brilliant investment banker and strategist. He had served on the advisory council of two U.S. Secretaries of the Treasury and was a personal friend and confidant of several sitting members of Federal Reserve board. He had served as CEO of several companies in the high tech, telecommunications, manufacturing and financial services industries. Like Willis, he was also focused on hard numbers and was leaning heavily on Fagan to grow Unidigitel, fix its cost structure, and turn things around quickly after the debacle with Forrester.

Schultz had made it clear to Ms. Fagan that bringing in Charlie was her one shot to turn things around. He was supportive of the investment in her mentor and his plans, but had said to her many times "If Charlie is the guy who can fix this, you need to show me how it's going to happen." Upon their first meeting, he said the same words to Charlie and made it clear that he would have little tolerance for budget overruns or missed deadlines. This time, he assured Charlie, he'd be watching this so-called transformation program with the scrutiny of a Las Vegas floor boss.

As Charlie stood in the elevator, waiting for the numbers to change from "Express" to the mid-30s where it would begin to stop on the various executive floors, he was not wholly confident in his relationship with Schultz. The man was resistant to Charlie's overtures to get to know him better. When they spent time together one-on-one, Schultz typically grilled him about budgets, deadlines and progress, allowing no personal or casual conversation to detract from the business discussion.

Charlie had invited Schultz to join him for a round of golf at Pebble Beach, for a tee time he'd happened to reserve 10 months before joining Unidigitel. But Schultz, who had once qualified for the U.S. Open as an amateur, patently refused, explaining that he wasn't in the business of being Charlie's buddy. Dowd assumed this was not for any personal reasons, but rather because Schultz understood the personal relationship between Fagan and Dowd. Schultz saw their fates as being intertwined and wanted no emotional interference should the day come that he'd have to crucify the two of them in the media for undermining Unidigitel's market position.

Charlie was heading into his meeting with the Board to sell his story and gain their support. His message was that the program needed additional investment and more time to progress, not only because of how badly Forrester had derailed it, but because of the inevitable hiccups that accompanied programs of this scope and scale. Though Charlie knew he had begun to foster change; had some early cost and revenue benefits to share; and had earned the respect and cooperation of many key individuals and groups throughout the company, he was also insecure about some assumptions he'd made early on. He hadn't properly anticipated the impact of change-resistance across the company, ran into some difficult supplier issues along the way, and was delayed by a data quality quagmire that was stickier, more time consuming, and more expensive to overcome than anyone could see until it became a central issue.

The elevator stopped at the 34th floor, and as the doors opened Charlie saw a friendly and familiar face looking a bit ruddy and tired, as if the previous night's sleep was fitful at best and the anticipated stress of the upcoming meeting was building quickly. The top of Marc Miller's balding head revealed a slight sheen of sweat, and Charlie noticed he was tugging at his own tie, as Dowd had done while waiting for the elevator.

Miller, the man Charlie had appointed as his Program Management Officer – and thus his chief lieutenant – forced a smile, shook Charlie's hand and said; "now I know how Louis the sixteenth felt walking towards the guillotine with thousands of Frenchman screaming for his head." Charlie couldn't help but emit a nervous chortle as the elevator doors closed and the car began to rise again toward the top floor. Leave it to Miller to be brutally honest and inappropriately funny at any opportunity.

Dos and Don'ts for Chapter 1	
DO:	**DON'T:**
Communicate continually, to the point of over-communication, with all stakeholders and the Board.	Assume people automatically want to change to something "better".
Recognize that a Senior IT Manager's role is part change agent.	Think that merely completing a series of technical implementations or tasks will lead to success.
Build trust and relationships by listening to people at all levels of the organization.	Obscure facts or hide negative information.
Continually seek to simplify.	Fail to involve impacted business owners and stakeholders from outside of IT.
Address bad news early and don't shoot the messenger.	Make people afraid to deliver bad news by punishing them for it.

For more information on how EMC Consulting can assist you with your transformation visit: - **www.emc.com/services**

CHAPTER 2

Marc Miller was smart, friendly, and quick to use humor to diffuse tension. Though often accused of being cynical, he considered himself a realist. This disputed personality characteristic was one of his strengths as a program manager. One of his favorite professional sayings, which had become something of a mantra during the past year, was "every day you have to ask yourself what can go wrong that can derail the program?'" And in his 22 years working on major IT projects, he'd seen an awful lot go wrong because managers overlooked certain details. Those who could anticipate trouble were the managers he most sought to emulate as he had advanced in his career.

Charlie Dowd brought "Miller," as most of his colleagues knew him, to Unidigitel during his second week as CIO. They'd worked closely together at Charlie's previous post, so Dowd had it in mind to try to bring Miller onto his team as soon as he began to think he'd take Liz Fagan up on her offer. Miller was the program manager who for three years had helped him to steer the ultimately successful program around some massive but submerged icebergs that would have otherwise sunk it. At the time, Miller was working for a major systems integrator, as he had for the past decade. He wasn't being granted partner status though because he was too busy doing what he did best – getting his hands dirty on projects that were in severe jeopardy.

While his more politically interested colleagues were busy taking on "the easy stuff" so that they could network their way up the ladder, Miller was traveling back and forth to places like Mumbai, Kuala Lumpur and Manila doing the kind of work most partners wanted to avoid. When Charlie Dowd offered him the position as his chief program manager, he scrutinized the well publicized situation, but was intrigued nonetheless. He trusted Charlie implicitly and liked the idea of staying stateside for awhile and spending more time with his family. "I'll need to give a few weeks notice," Miller told Charlie when he called to tell him he'd accept his offer, "but I'm on the beach anyway right now and they owe me about a century of vacation time, so expect me in California on June 1st."

His decision to make this move was not because he was a casualty of mass layoffs or because he wanted to move out of IT. Instead it was because he had learned that IT technology was essentially useless if it didn't serve the businesses' needs. He wanted to understand the language of the business people he'd come to work with more closely as a project manager and architect. After earning his MBA at the University of Chicago, he was recruited to the major systems integration house that ultimately made him a program manager and eventually brought him into contact with Charlie Dowd.

A critical lesson Miller credited Charlie with teaching him was that one of a program manager's most important jobs was to prioritize continually the massive list of activities that a program could take on in theory, but could never accomplish all at once in reality. Miller was skilled at vendor and personnel selection before he met Charlie, but took his abilities to the next level observing Dowd as he excelled at getting the most from his software vendors through a combination of performance-based contracts and various motivational and competitive techniques.

Upon joining Unidigitel, Miller knew he wasn't going to be given a year to make something happen. Charlie had explained to him that his first two months would be spent assembling the rest of his core program management team; auditing the heck out of all of the program's existing and past activities; and deliver a new go-forward strategy that would put the program, and ultimately the entire IT organization, back on track. Miller set a checkpoint for himself and was determined that by three months from his start date he would know exactly how deep "Forrester's crevasse" went and would have a team, a plan, and some momentum to climb out of it.

"Forrester's Crevasse" would become something of an unofficial title for the program. Ultimately, his team would embrace it so well that they began decorating Miller's office with bits of climbing gear, cross country skiing kit, and posters of everything from polar bears to the Patagonian ice fields. Miller was so focused on interviewing business owners and building consensus among the executives in his first six weeks that it wasn't until one of his lieutenants placed a mannequin dressed as a Sherpa just inside his office doorway late one night that he realized the cult-following his sarcastic nickname had created. He figured it was good for team morale, so he hung one of his old name badges from a trade show around the Sherpa's neck and left the dummy where it stood.

What Miller understood clearly within his first month working for Charlie was that Forrester's plan was far more than any IT group could handle, particularly without any outside help or an effective program management office to keep all of the efforts synchronized. Miller discovered that Forrester had actually tried to rework his plans into a two year schedule. Year one would focus on the architecture build out. Year two would focus on product and customer migration. While this seemed reasonable to Forrester on paper, it was still an overly ambitious road map. Even if the scope hadn't been too large, and his best of breed approach wasn't flawed, his other mistakes – like failing to engage business owners, create a realistic risk plan, or engage an executive steering committee – would ultimately have doomed it to fail.

Miller had to devise a new plan and nail down what was realistic to accomplish in one year, starting at about 60 days from his hire date. This plan wouldn't deliver the program's entire vision, but would move things forward pragmatically and deliver some short term wins. Part of his effort needed to focus on assembling an effective team of people from within and from outside the company. Charlie and Miller worked together to develop an organizational structure that they knew, from past experience, could be effective.

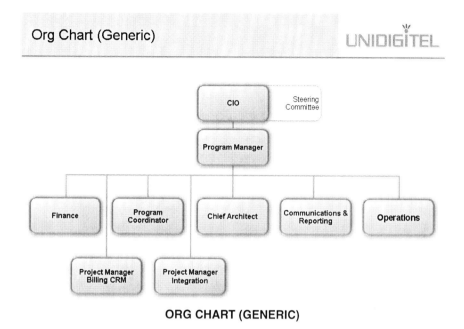

ORG CHART (GENERIC)

This team's jobs would include an intense discovery phase to determine the current status of the program and the reasons for its problems. It would then have to realign the program's goals with the business' needs; revise or rewrite the requirements; rein in the budget; assess and manage ongoing risks; and establish an effective adoption management structure. It would also have to manage change with strict discipline and define ways to measure incremental benefits at key check points.

Finding the right people, while navigating some internal politics, was going to be tricky. Miller's challenge was to find people inside the company who could be effective, weren't already burned out, and who were perhaps misused under Forrester. Folks who were already exhausted, couldn't be salvaged, or who had one foot out the door likely would not get the job done. Miller knew some key people from outside of the company he wanted to bring onto the team, but the whole team couldn't consist of outsiders. Even skilled outsiders wouldn't have enough familiarity with Unidigitel's inner workings to meet the truncated time frames the program faced. Miller's team had to be able to determine what the right "small bites" to take up front might be that would deliver the greatest benefits and be the most feasible to accomplish.

Charlie and Miller also did not want to create a mercenary atmosphere – or appear to be doing so - where experts with many different career opportunities in front of them would work for hire, but never really commit themselves to overcoming the program's major challenges for Unidigitel's sake. Miller's team would have to combine insiders and newcomers who had critical skill sets and the right attitude to make the program succeed. He would also need to reevaluate and reengage all of the software vendors; shed several of the moving parts from Forrester's architecture; restructure contracts and bonuses based on performance milestones; and twist arms to get the vendors to bring their best people – their 'A' teams – back to the program.

From day one, Miller's first choice for his right hand man was Jim Taylor. An expert in program governance and structure, Jim had worked side by side with Miller on dozens of programs for the past seven years. Miller liked to describe Jimmy, as he'd call his friend to tease him, a bit like mouthwash – you hate the taste, but you have to use it. Taylor wasn't unrelenting, but he was detailed oriented and never hesitated to call people out when they missed key deadlines and didn't report status correctly. "Don't tell me you're almost done," he'd say. "You're either done, or you're in the red. Tell it to me straight." Taylor could play a key role where he would effectively take the program's temperature and keep Miller and Charlie up to speed on what was and wasn't happening day to day.

Ultimately it would take more than an attractive compensation package and a boat load of perks to bring Taylor in. He wasn't unhappy in his current position, though he wasn't especially challenged. Miller knew that he thrived on projects that were hitting the wall, and could tend to lose interest when things were going smoothly. He was bound to be excited by the fixer-upper that was Unidigitel's ailing transformation program. Taylor flew to California for a day from his home in Charlotte, North Carolina to meet with Miller and Charlie face to face. Ultimately, it wasn't Miller's taunts that convinced him to sign on. It was the opportunity to learn from Charlie Dowd and focus on one Herculean project that captured his interest.

While Miller had been cajoling Taylor, he also searched for a chief architect. Though he had some former colleagues in mind, he decided that this spot needed to be filled from the inside if it could be. He'd come across a potential candidate somewhat by chance. While glancing through a pile of status reports organized by date from the Forrester days in his first week, he noticed that the first few in the sequence had been submitted by one person, but the rest had Forrester's name on them. He'd heard that Forrester was controlling, and that many of his reports proved not to be completely accurate. But the first few were exacting in their detail, and subtly scathing in their criticism of Forrester's methods.

A quick check with HR told him that the person who'd written these reports, a man named Earl Campbell, was still with the company. He was now working in a limited role, managing a small team on an obscure project in a location where, frankly, a number of folks who were approaching retirement age had essentially been sent out to pasture. Campbell was in his late fifties and it was clear to Miller that he was detail oriented, critical, concise and brutally honest. Hoping Campbell wasn't simply killing time until retirement, Miller decided to call him and hear his story.

"Scanning systems, this is Earl Campbell," said the slightly bitter voice at the other end of Marc Miller's phone.

"Mr. Campbell, this is Marc Miller. I'm not sure if you know who I am, but…"

"Yeah, I heard of you," Campbell said sharply, cutting Miller off. "You're the new guy running that mess of a program they've got going on over there. Look, I've already been blamed for half of what's going wrong, so you might want to find someone else to point fingers at. I'm not playing that game anymore."

"Okay…" Miller said, wondering if he'd confirmed what conventional wisdom says about making assumptions, "but hear me out for a minute. I saw a few status reports with your name on them. You might know more about this effort than anyone in the company. I don't know how you ended up where you are now, but I'll bet based on these reports that Forrester didn't like you because you weren't playing things his way. Is that about right?"

"You're close," Campbell said. "I don't take kindly to young, hot headed idiots making life miserable for people I've worked with for a decade. Bradley didn't like it when I told him he was setting himself up to fail. He got a little upset when I filed those reports you have there – especially when I said there was no way his year one plan would work, even if we had twice as many people and three times the budget. I think what really cheesed him off though was when I emailed Liz Fagan to tell her she was going to have a mutiny on her hands because he wouldn't listen to anybody. That's when Bradley voted me off the island and sent me here."

"Well, Mr. Campbell…"

"Call me Earl. Everyone else does."

"Okay, Earl. I think he made a pretty big mistake and I want to know if you're ready to jump back in and help us make this thing work they way it's supposed to."

Campbell gave out a lengthy exhale – a sigh that said "aw heck" and "you've got to be kidding me" all at once. After a moment he replied. "I'll tell you what Mr. Miller. I've been in this business for about 30 years. I've been everything from a requirements analyst and programmer to a lead architect. In all of that time, I've never seen a program so badly managed or met someone as arrogant as Bradley Forrester."

"Well, I assure you…"

"I'm not finished," he cut Miller off again. "I read about Charlie Dowd. I know – Annapolis grad, made a name for himself with whatever bank that was, and all that. I've even heard from some of my pals that he's not a complete jerk. And I also heard that so far you seem to be alright and have some clue of what you're doing, though I can't figure why you'd leave a cushy job for this mess. I'd like to help you out, if for no other reason than my stock will be worth more when I retire if this thing succeeds. But I'll tell you what – if you want someone who's gonna go along and get along, you might as well hang up right now. I'm not that guy."

"Actually, I'm looking for someone who'll…"

"Yeah, I know, you want someone who'll talk straight and tell it like it is…sure, sure. But tell me this – what makes you think you can fix this thing? Do you really know how deep it goes?"

Miller said nothing.

"You gonna answer me?"

"You gonna cut me off again?"

"Nope."

Miller was irritated, but engaged. "Well, I didn't call you because I'm looking for someone to tell me what they think I want to hear, or because I think I can fix it or because I already know how deep it goes. But I'm guessing *you* might," Miller retorted. " And I think you know who else in this company has a shot at making it work. It won't get fixed unless we get some people involved who don't mess around and who know this company. Sound right to you?"

"Yeah. Actually, that does sound about right. I'm almost pleasantly surprised to hear you say that…Mr. Miller."

"Alright, well, why don't we get together later this week and get started."

"Wasting no time. Sounds good."

"Good, but one other thing - call me Miller. Everyone else does."

"How's Thursday at 2?" Campbell asked him.

"Good. I'm in the main building, 32nd floor."

Poor requirements were one of the biggest problems the program faced. The original requirements Forrester created simply weren't aligned with the business. They then drifted over time as Forrester chased new solutions and technical approaches he'd found interesting. He was knowledgeable enough to bring in a world-class billing vendor that had a reputation for never having had a failed implementation. But it seemed to Miller that his main issue was that he didn't have the experience or ability to run either a program or an IT organization of this scale. He tinkered rather than planned. He talked rather than listened. After nearly six months of constant requirements changes that seemed to have little consistency, his vendors became frustrated and wanted to distance themselves from what was a distracting and problematic project.

The "A" teams that some of the key vendors originally assigned to this ambitious and lucrative program were gradually replaced by "B" and "C" teams so top talent could be re-assigned where the vendors needed them more. Miller knew he had to get the vendors re-engaged. He would need to bring back as much "A" talent as he could. Further, the vendors needed to be more accountable for the success, or failure, of the overall program. In short, they needed to have more skin in the game.

The only way he'd pull this off would be to regain their confidence. This would begin, he felt, with requirements that made sense, performance milestones that were achievable, and requirements change processes that let the vendors know the program wouldn't change direction without notice, logic, or consensus. Developing new requirements and new requirements processes were therefore necessary for the program to move forward in a healthy way.

Before they'd seen a single chart or report, Charlie and Miller suspected that Forrester's architecture involved too many moving parts. Jim Taylor agreed with their assessment at first glance. On paper, Forrester's architecture was elegant and impressive. In reality, however, it was impractical. In his first week with Unidigitel Charlie had actually managed to get Forrester on the phone briefly in an effort to understand the man's initial vision. All he learned, however, was that Forrester still felt he'd been trying to do the right things. He believed he'd selected the very best technologies but had been railroaded by the business owners who couldn't understand his solution approach.

Jim and Miller had seen plenty of CIOs and architects make Forrester's mistakes. He'd bet it all on technology but didn't have an effective plan for moving the mammoth company to that technology. He'd also failed to acknowledge that major IT conversions were like a three-legged stool. One leg was always technology, but people and processes were just as, if not more, important. In a large organization like Unidigitel, it wasn't possible to start from a clean slate. Even in a massive conversion like this one, the best that could be done would be to improve on what was in place rather than replacing everything with what looked best on paper. By failing to account for people and processes, Forrester failed to account for Unidigitel's culture and embedded complexity.

To accommodate this complexity and reduce risk, Charlie and Miller planned to simplify the architecture. Simplification would help them to recover the runaway program. They knew that reducing the number of piece parts overall would rein in the scope, cut out significant integration costs, and reduce the number of variables that had to be managed. They'd seen in previous programs how "best of breed approaches" involved too much customization. The approach would often aim to bring together distinct functional components that could meet the greatest number of granular requirements in each specific area. But this functional myopia sacrificed speed, cost containment and seamlessness for piece parts that were individually strong, but required significant development work to come together as a whole. In the long run, even a successful implementation could prove inflexible and extremely expensive to maintain.

Charlie and Miller took that approach that fewer components might not hit every detailed functional requirement, but they didn't need to. They just needed to get the job done well enough. It was more important that they were stable, performed well together, and didn't require massive amounts of custom integration and long term maintenance cost and effort. In order to reduce the number of components, however, Miller and his team would need to determine which pieces of Forrester's original architecture could remain and take on more responsibilities, which would be minimized, and which would be written off completely. New business requirements were needed to help guide their decisions.

These new requirements had to reflect improved and re-engineered processes that gave business owners and users tools that made them more effective. But Charlie, Miller and Jim also agreed that customizing the solution to meet every business need was not likely to be feasible or cost effective. At some level, the business' needs had to intersect with or even adapt to the solution's capabilities. This is where a lot of give and take with different business owners would come into play. There would be situations where the new solution could deliver what business owners wanted, just in a different way than they might have wished.

Jim's job, among other things, would be to recommend the best ways to make the new solutions meet the business' needs. In doing so, he would have to prevent scope creep from happening as Charlie and Miller worked to appease business owners and earn their support. Earl Campbell's knowledge of the IT organizations inner workings, and those of the various business units, would prove invaluable to this part of Taylor's job.

"What you guys are talking about is what I'd call a mall strategy," Campbell told Charlie, Miller, and Jim as they worked together to revise the program's architecture plan.

"How's that?" Miller asked, interested but not recognizing the metaphor immediately.

"Well, Brad did the stupid thing and tried to find the best component for every function. But we all know that approach can be a real bear to implement. What can work in a situation like this though, where you're going to need three or four different vendors to cover the whole scope, is to choose one to be the anchor – like an anchor store in a mall."

Everyone nodded, now understanding the reference.

"Right, so what you're saying is that we figure out which combination of vendor and solution can handle the most real estate best and make that company the main 'throat to choke'?" Jim added.

"Now you're on the trolley Jimmy," Campbell said with a smirk. "And I think what we're starting to see here is that the anchor should be the biller. That vendor can handle our scope, and I suspect their solution can cover most of the CRM and product catalog requirements."

"If it can, we eliminate a few big pieces right away," Taylor said.

"Exactly," Campbell continued. "Miller, you'd need to get some of their best people back in here to make it work. Plus, the guy you really want to run that piece of the program is Al Marcus. He's their ace manager. I'm not sure how you get him here, but I do know all of their project managers think he's a miracle worker. They all wished he'd been here before, because they figured he would have taken on Bradley. And when those guys started being transferred, most of them put in to be moved to Al's team, even though he was off on some project in Asia. That should tell you something about him."

"I think I've met him actually," Miller said. "Only briefly, but I know of him by reputation at least. He's got this sort of aura with all the telecom guys from our old company that worked with him in Australia two years ago."

Al Marcus had a reputation in telecom IT circles as a sort of genius. He seemed to have that magic touch where every project he'd led turned to gold. He was highly intelligent, a real problem solver and someone who seemed to have endless amounts of both energy and patience. In truth, he was simply an experienced and charismatic manager. He was a listener who understood how to motivate individuals. Further, he was willing to stick to his guns when others would fold under pressure or give in organization politics.

Those who'd worked with Al appreciated his positive encouragement, but knew that his calm and cold way of expressing disappointment was something they wanted to avoid. People would run through walls for Al Marcus, or so Miller had heard. When Miller emailed the account rep for Commapps, the billing vendor, the reply he received told him flatly that Al just wasn't available. He was working on a major account in Singapore. The rep hyped up several other potential managers as being "just as good". Miller thanked her for the information as he replied from his Blackberry, and immediately dialed up Charlie Dowd.

"What's up Marc?" Charlie said on the other end of the line. The two remained in constant contact, so it was no surprise for Charlie to hear from his chief lieutenant.

"I need a favor…" Miller said.

"Okay…what's the problem?"

"Well, we want Al Marcus right?"

"You can't get him?"

"I can't. But I'm thinking you can. And since it's your job to get me what I need so I can cover your backside, I figure you'll probably get it done."

"You're funny. Let me see what I can do. I know one of Commapp's board members and he owes me a few favors."

Later that afternoon, Charlie reviewed an email from Miller about Al Marcus and what the account rep had said. A few calls to trusted sources told him that Marcus appeared to be what Earl Campbell originally said about him – he was a veteran, an expert, and impressively accomplished at delivering the Commapps billing solution in large scale accounts. The program he was running in Singapore was going smoothly and nearing completion. He suspected that Marcus himself would want to bring it over the finish line, making it unlikely he would agree to start something new from scratch, especially a program as flawed as Unidigitel's.

Undaunted, Charlie dropped a note to John Bettis, a member of Commapps' board with whom he'd worked closely on several projects a decade earlier. Bettis was a West Point graduate with whom Charlie had a standing $100 bet on the annual Army-Navy football game. After the 2006 season, Navy had won five in a row, including a 34-6 drubbing that stood among the most lopsided beatings in the history of the series. Going into the 2007 game, the notoriously stingy Bettis had yet to pay Charlie a red nickel, but blanched at any suggestion that he'd ultimately welch on what he owed. Charlie had ribbed him about it, sending him emails featuring Fred, Navy's mascot goat, giving the Army Black Night butts to the backside. In a moment of brashness, Bettis replied to Charlie with three simple words, "double or nothing." Charlie took the bet. Navy whipped Army 38-3. Bettis owed Charlie a cool grand.

"John, Charlie Dowd calling," Charlie said as Bettis answered his cell phone.

"I was wondering when I'd hear from you. It's been seven months. How much do I owe you? Is it $600 now?"

"Try $1000…but you can keep the money. I need a favor. I need you to get me a guy named Al Marcus. He's an ace delivery guy…"

"Yeah, I know Al pretty well. He *is* an ace."

"Well, he's tied up on a project, but I need him."

"When?"

"Immediately. Yesterday. The next flight back would be ideal."

"Well, I need to make some phone calls, but I'll try to have him in your office within two weeks or so. How's that?"

"It'll have to do. That's much appreciated."

"So this makes us even then." It wasn't a question.

"Yeah, until we whip the cadets again in the fall."

Bettis chuckled. "Get ready to owe me one. Tell the wife I send my regards."

"Likewise. Talk to you soon."

On a Monday in late July, a few days after Al Marcus had arrived from Singapore, Charlie invited him to an early breakfast at his favorite diner. He wanted to catch Marcus off balance if he could by taking him out of his element – that of first class flights and expensive European restaurants – and talk to him in the midst of pure Americana. They met at the greasy spoon at 7:30 am on a Wednesday. A few of the regulars in the diner cast sidelong glances at the slick haired Brit in the Italian suit who'd just sauntered in before turning back to their coffee and bacon.

"You're going to ask me for something very uncomfortable, aren't you Charles?" Marcus said without betraying a hint of emotion. His reputation for being unflappable remained intact thus far. "Come out with it then, eh?"

"You already know the good news Al, that we're planning to give you the entire CRM area as well as the product catalog migration project."

"Yes, which is why I am certain you have some sort of bad news for me."

"I wouldn't call it bad news. I just think we need to get a few things straight. See, you're part of my team now, aren't you?"

"I'd like to think so. But that doesn't mean I'm a patsy."

"No, not at all, but I'll need a few things from you."

Al nodded expectantly.

"I've been looking at the personnel from Commapps who are staffing the project. What I can see is that when this thing started, Unidigitel had mostly 'A' people. But as this thing started to sink, they were replaced with what I suspect are B guys, and maybe Cs in some cases. I want your 'A' team back. We're about to break the news to Rick Williams that his CRM contract is being terminated, but that doesn't mean we can't change course."

"There's no need for threats Charlie. I know who I want on this project with me. I'm not being hung out to dry on my own product because I have a team of rookies working for me."

"I'm glad to hear that. You should also know that when we contract for the CRM and product catalog pieces, I'm going to insist that every payment be tied to a specific milestone. Miller can talk to you more about what those are. Plus, the bonus structure for the whole program will be interdependent. Everyone's bonuses will be tied to everyone meeting the schedule successfully."

"We make our deadlines Charlie. I don't really see why you'd need to go a step further there…"

"I'll tell you why," Charlie interceded. "I don't want any finger pointing coming from anyone. I want to know that if someone else starts falling behind, your best people are going to step up to get us over the hump. You might be getting the biggest piece of the business, but that also means I'll expect more from you and your people than from anyone else. And by your people I also mean the folks from Rick's team who will join yours."

"I'm not sure we need them Charlie…"

"I'm sure you do. Those guys know the existing databases and processes better than anyone in the company and we don't have 3 months for your 'A' team to come back in and figure it out. You're going to depend on these guys for some local knowledge and I want to make sure everyone plays nicely."

"I see, and I have one request from you then."

"What's that?"

"That you draw very specific lines around what we do, actually what each of the vendors will do, and make it clear that crossing those boundaries, or chipping away at our footprint, will not be tolerated. I don't want to walk in here one morning and find Williams eating off my plate."

"You don't need to worry about turf wars AI. They interfere with the schedule. As long as your folks meet their commitments, we won't have any problems."

"Okay, then I only have one more question for you."

"Ask away."

"How are the Huevos Rancheros? I didn't sleep very well last night and could use something with a kick to get me going today."

"An iron stomach to go along with your iron will. I like it. You'd have done well in the Navy."

"I don't do boats Charlie. Haven't you ever seen *Titanic*?"

Miller liked Earl Campbell, though he wasn't ready to admit that yet. Campbell was a little mouthy, bordering on rude, and had a profound grasp of expletives. But he was obsessive about detail and was proving in his first two weeks on Miller's team to be a huge help. Campbell understood how Unidigitel was constructed, who the real players were, and what exactly Forrester had done wrong.

With Campbell aboard, Miller's team was coming together. His first real meeting of the minds was about 10 days away, but Miller still hadn't found the person who'd handle user adoption. He'd sat down with several project managers who all had solid project management skills, but none of them had the network within the company or the personality needed to convince the user community to embrace the coming changes. Miller knew that even a program that was managed right and hit all of its deadlines could fail in the end if the users didn't support it. Pulling them in early on, making them feel included, and soliciting their feedback in the requirements process was absolutely necessary for long term success. He needed someone who had the management skills for the job, to whom the users could relate personally, and who'd been through the past year with them and still had a good reputation. He asked Campbell for his opinion.

Campbell flipped through a file of names and notes on a number of candidates from across the company. He knew them all and didn't hesitate to provide a running commentary.

"Ben Watson? Too young. Too technical. And he's one of those kids that text messages all the time. It irritates me. Next."

"Vijay Mahadweshar? He's a smart kid, but the kind you lock in the closet and tell him to de-bug code. Business guys would chew him up. Next."

"Jennifer Schwartz. She's smart and pretty tough, but she just left on maternity leave. Too bad really, she'd be useful somewhere in this. So, next…"

"Bob Randolph," Campbell snickered. "Randolph couldn't find his rear end with two hands and a map. Spends most of his time kissing up…Bradley liked him. I'm not sure how we survived the purge. I'll admit he manages to look good on paper, but he's about as useful as a fish hook on a duck hunt. Miller, you got anyone *good* for me to look at?"

"That's about all I have. I was going to…"

"How about Parma Singh?"

"I don't know her…"

"She's sharp, and tough, but charming. She's not as experienced as some of these others, but she knows her stuff. We worked together for a while and I was impressed with her. You'd like her Miller. She'd let you finish your sentences."

"When do you think…"

"I'll reach out to her. She still works downstairs. I think she's keeping ordering up and running while everything else is burning to the ground around her. She could probably use a change of pace."

It was 8:30 am on Monday, July 21st. Parma Singh was sitting in her cube in front of her laptop, wondering if this was the day she'd have an email from HR asking her to stop by. Several of her colleagues had already been let go as the new group of IT managers began collapsing extraneous projects to rein the budget in. When she opened her email inbox, she saw a name she didn't expect: Earl Campbell.

With curiosity she opened the message. It read,

Parma-
Worried? Don't be. I may have something you would be great for. Please gimme a call when you get this. Hope you've been doing well despite the turmoil.
Earl

Parma had worked briefly for Earl as a project manager nearly a year earlier, before he was pushed aside for challenging Brad Forrester. Many people didn't like his gruff and sarcastic way, but he never seemed to unleash it on Parma. She had enjoyed the discussions they shared about technology and strategies for managing teams of developers. She had always thought of him as an unofficial mentor.

She didn't know it, but Earl thought she had more management potential than anyone who worked for him. He'd always intended to give her a break if ever given the chance. His cell number was still in her phone. She decided to call him later in the morning, after she'd cleared her inbox and figured he'd have had a few cups of coffee.

"This is Earl," Campbell said, his raw voice seemingly forcing its way out of Parma's phone.

"Mr. Campbell, its Parma Singh."

"Parma! Hey, so you got my email. How've you been?" Parma had always called him Mr. Campbell. He'd asked her to call him Earl many times before and she just wouldn't do it, so he'd given up. He wouldn't admit that he actually liked it.

"I've been alright. Just trying to focus on my work. Admittedly I've been expecting a note from HR. I was surprised to see your name in my inbox."

"Well, I'm glad you called. I have an opportunity for you. I'm unlikely to take no for an answer."

"Yes, well, I wouldn't expect any less. How can I help you?"

"It hasn't been announced too loudly yet, but I'm now the chief architect for this program."

"Congratulations," she replied.

"We're trying to pull it out of a nose dive," he pressed on, "so I'm involved in putting together the program management office. We need someone who knows how the company works, has some cachet with the middle management folks and front line users, and who's organized and gets things done."

"Well, Mr. Campbell, I could try to make some recommendations."

"Parma, please, I'm talking about you. I want you to take on the adoption management role for the PMO. I'd like to introduce you to Marc Miller, the new program manager, and to Charlie Dowd, the new CIO. I think you're the right person for this job."

"I'm...flattered," she replied with some surprise in her voice. "I've been expecting to be moving on, not promoted."

"Ms. Singh, we've got some weak players in this company. You ain't one of them. Let me get you together with Marc, and also with Jim Taylor, and they'll bring you on board."

"I'm not sure what to say. Thank you, Mr. Campbell. This is a great opportunity."

"You've earned it. But don't thank me yet. You may curse me in a few weeks when you see what's involved in this thing...Listen, I need to run to another call. I'll talk to you later today or tomorrow and get you connected to Marc. Take care Parma."

"You too Mr. Campbell."

As Parma walked into Marc Miller's office, in the afternoon of the following day, she stopped short and unintentionally gaped at the mannequin in the doorway. She took two steps into the room without taking her eyes off this curiosity. When she realized she hadn't introduced herself to anyone, she turned a shade of pink and took a step backwards.

Miller, Al, and Earl began to laugh immediately.

"That's the Sherpa. You can say hello later," Marc Miller said while standing and extending a hand for Parma to shake. "I'm Marc Miller."

"It's a pleasure to meet you Mr. Miller. I'm Parma."

"Most people just call me Miller."

"Don't bother," Earl intruded from across the room. "She'll call you 'mister' whether you prefer it or not."

"Why don't you come in and have a seat and we'll talk a bit about what we have in store for you here."

Parma was introduced to Al Marcus, who was his usual polite self, and she greeted Earl Campbell with a smile as she sat in one of the oddly matched swivel chairs strewn about the office. On the wall behind Miller's desk was a whiteboard choked with architectural drawings, arrows, notes, and remnants of previous drawings and notes. On the wall next to the desk were photos of Miller's family, a map of California with notes written on it, and a growing collection of images of mountain climbers and explorers hastily tacked into the drywall that Jim and Earl had been collecting and hanging when Miller wasn't looking.

"Parma, I don't think I need to get too deep into the details on what adoption management means, but that'll be your area. We'll need you to help engage the various user communities while we redefine all of the requirements. You'll be in charge of the focus groups we need for that, for testing, and ultimately for rolling the new stuff out. You'll be heavily involved in managing change requests and in running workshops to get the middle manager and users on board with the idea that we can do a lot for them. Al here will help you to understand all of that and can backstop you, as can Jim and I, if the business folks throw anything your way that just isn't feasible or aligned with the rest of our plan. You'll work with all of us, but you'll work most closely with Al and Charlie."

This last point took Parma a second to accept. She'd be working directly with the CIO. It wasn't something she'd expected, but she realized immediately that she was being put in a position of considerable influence, and as such more responsibility than she'd ever quite managed before.

"Parma," Campbell stepped in, "obviously there's a lot of activity happening. But we see your role as spanning the entire three year program. So, you'll be working on the user acceptance testing, on roll outs probably in multiple phases, and in introducing new releases to the different user communities. In other words, from the requirements to the delivery of this thing – soup to nuts – you'll be central to the success of this."

Parma shot him a look that said, "are you sure I'm right for this?"

"Don't worry," he said. "I wouldn't have vouched for you if I didn't know you can handle this. And you'll have me, and these fellas, and Charlie to back you up."

Parma wrinkled her brow at this. She knew Forrester. He was an egoist who kept to himself. She didn't realize Charlie was a hands-on guy who liked to help and teach people around him.

"When Charlie comes back to town in a few days," Miller told her, "we'll have you two spend some time working together and getting your plans in order. You'll find him to be a great ally in this. He might be the boss, but he's taking on the business alignment piece, so he's really one of us in the context of the program."

This sounded encouraging to Parma, but she still wasn't sure she believed it.

"In the meantime," Miller continued, "let's take a few hours to walk you through what we know now, what our next steps are, and who'll be doing what. Al and Earl can speak to the vendor components we're re-evaluating, we'll give you a good summary of what's coming out of the discovery phase we're working on, and we'll answer any questions you have along the way. Sound good?"

"Yes it does Mr. Miller. It's a bit overwhelming just now," she smiled, "But, I'm ready to get started," she said. She pulled a notebook and Indian gold pen from her leather satchel, adjusted her stylish glasses, and wrote the date at the top of the blank page.

"Good. We need you to get up to speed right away and start laying out a plan of attack for how you want to manage your piece of the program," Miller said. He shot Campbell a look that said, "Sharp pick. This one's a winner." Miller was proceeding with Parma as though she'd earn the job. In reality, he was evaluating her and knew it was early enough in the process to replace her if necessary. Thus far, however, she had made an excellent impression.

On a Wednesday morning, the last in July, the entire group – including Miller, Jim, Al, Earl, and Parma - gathered for the first time in a small conference room near Miller's messy office. Each of the individuals had met previously, but we're still getting to know each other. Sitting around a conference table that was just a touch too large for the room, everyone chatted as Miller fiddled with the projector and his PC, readying the presentation he needed to give to make everyone's assignments and marching orders crystal clear. Campbell and Marcus were trading good natured barbs while Taylor and Singh small talked about their families, where they'd gone to school, and how they'd become involved in the program. The team was mixing well without encouragement, so Miller took his time with the A/V gear and let the conversation run on for a bit. He was brought up short by Campbell's sharpened tongue.

"Hey Miller, how do you expect us to believe you can run this ship if you can't get a projector to work."

Miller popped the lens cap off the buzzing machine and his opening slide appeared on the screen. For once, Campbell shut his mouth and nodded to Miller in a veiled sign of submission.

"Okay everyone," Miller began. You all know roughly why you're here, but I'd like to get into a bit of detail about next steps; everyone's roles; and critical aspects of this program that we need to change or improve."

The first slide Miller displayed was his organizational

chart, now populated with the names of the key players on the team.

"This first slide should demonstrate to everyone how the

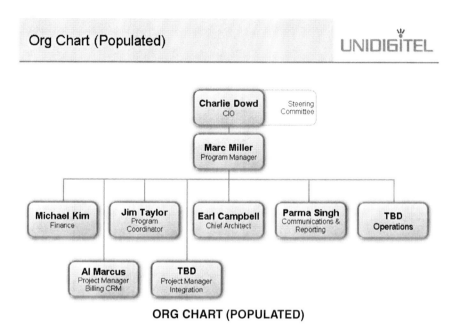

Org Chart (Populated)   UNIDIGITEL

ORG CHART (POPULATED)

reporting structure will work for our team. The two boxes with TBD are roles we still need to fill. The integration project manager will come from our system's integration, though Charlie, Jim and I are still working through the details there. The operations manager, we hope, will come from somewhere within Unidigitel, though we're still looking for good candidates there," he explained.

As Miller progressed through his slides, he fleshed out more details of the program management structure make roles and responsibility clear to each member of the team. Miller himself would act as the Program Manager. He would be responsible for overall management of the program; reporting progress to Charlie Dowd; addressing everything from budget matters to requirements, architecture, and vendor issues; supporting the team in gaining the resources they needed to progress; and dealing with personnel issues and risks.

Charlie Dowd had agreed to take charge of Business

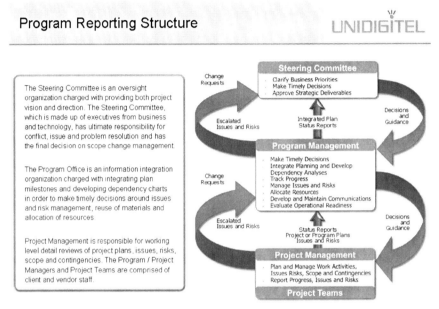

Program Reporting Structure

Alignment, the process of re-aligning the program's goals with those of the business. He would engage the managers, or business owners, who were responsible for telephony, internet and video sales and product management; wireless sales and product management; and order fulfillment, customer care, and billing in each domain. He would support Al Marcus and Parma Singh throughout the requirements gathering, change management, and user adoption management processes which would be guided by input from the business owners.

Dowd was also responsible for reporting progress to the Board of Directors and with Miller would establish a senior level steering committee to which major program issues could be escalated and dealt with. Miller stressed that Charlie would need the team's total support and commitment, especially because he and Charlie were slated to provide a clear assessment to the board at the 90 day mark, which was only about 50 days away.

"At this point," Miller informed the team, "I'm guessing that the project timeline will encompass a new three year plan; that we'll need anywhere from 10 to 30 percent more budget to get the job done" – at which point the team uttered a collective sigh while Campbell swore under his breath in agreement – "and we're going to go through some real pain to make process and organizational changes that have to be driven from the top down."

Jim Taylor would be in charge of the program's day to day functions from status reporting to escalating budget issues to reining in the scope. Most immediately, he would be responsible for putting a more robust program management structure in place, which would involve engaging a systems integrator, ITSI Consulting. He would have to define and establish the program's dependencies, which would be critical to Earl Campbell's risk management responsibilities, and vastly improve the PMO's ability to report status and anticipate problems.

As important, would be Taylor's ability to make people within the program feel empowered to do their jobs while creating a positive sense of urgency for everyone involved. This was a tall order in the wake of Forrester's mostly autocratic, second-guessing approach. Jim Taylor knew he had his work cut out for him, but his past experience told him that people in the organization would react positively to better communication, more useful structure, processes that made sense and visibility into status, dependencies, and progress across the program. One of the key assets he kept in his playbook was a communications matrix that he planned to institute. This matrix had helped him on many past projects and programs to define an overall communications plan and keep all of the information about how it worked in one place. This was particularly useful because of the tendency for communications plans to morph over time as projects, priorities, and scope changed and shifted.

Al Marcus would tackle solution requirements, bringing his

Communications Planning

The communication matrix is the centerpiece of the Communication Plan. It is deliberately designed so that all the information needed for managing the plan is located in one place.

Comm. Event / Artifact	Template	Content Provider	Trigger	Stakeholders	Distribution Channel	Archive	Comments
Status Report		Team Leaders	Weekly (Thursdays @ 5pm)	Program Manager	Email		
General Status Meeting		Program/Project Manager	Weekly (Fridays @ 9am)	Program	Meeting		Participants may dial in remotely
Status Meeting Minutes		Program/Project Manager	Weekly (next business day after status meeting @ 10am)	Program Stakeholders	Email		Participants dial in
Steering		Program		Steering			

TYPE	FORUM	AUDIENCE	PURPOSE	TOOLS
	One-on-One	Project Leader	• Review project status and milestones at a detailed level • Identify cross stream issues for escalation • Understand dependencies and resource constraints	• Status Report • Issue List
	Working Group	Area Leader	• Discuss cross stream dependencies • Review, resolve or escalate high and medium priority issues and all issues with cross-stream dependencies	• Status Report • Issue List • Working Group Pres.
	Steering Committee	Executive Sponsors	• Review high level summary of program and project status • Address all escalated issues	• Executive Dashboard • Steering Com. Pres.
	Requirements	Business Analysts	• Capture business requirements for inclusion by Project Leaders in Functional Design and Specifications	• N/A
	Staff Meeting	PMO Staff	• Communicate specific PMO information and updates • Address internal PMO issues and concerns	• N/A
	Town Hall	All	• Communicate consistent information to broad group • Address program wide concerns and major issues • Motivate team members	• N/A
	Portal	All	• Offer program and project status summaries, key announcements, contact lists and upcoming events • Archive and share documents • Provide reference site for new project members	• Shared Repository
	E-mail	Customized Group	• Provide more frequent and easily accessed information • Customize messages by audience	• Distribution Lists • Attachments
	Voicemail	Customized Group	• Send quick, urgent messages • Provide 'heads up'/alerts for other communications	• Distribution Lists

COMMUNICATIONS PLANNING

expertise with the core billing solution to the table and helping to translate between what Charlie said the business needed and the best way to get the solution to deliver it without massive customization. Marcus would have to work closely with Earl Campbell, the chief architect who had already done some of the major blocking and tackling of the revised solution approach with Miller.

Al would also have to help Parma Singh, who would handle adoption management. Parma could be in the line of fire between users, business owners and the program team as she collected feedback to feed into the change management process. Al and Jim Taylor would oversee that process, determining whether requests could be fulfilled, were not feasible, or simply weren't aligned with the program's business goals. When aggressive push back did occur, it would come from Al first and Jim second, but rarely from Parma who's job it was to engage and rally the user community, not to alienate it.

In addition to his architectural role, Earl Campbell would

have to establish strong risk management practices in relation to solutions development. Mostly this meant working with Jim Taylor to understand which of the program's dependencies were within their control, and which weren't. The latter represented risks that needed to be identified and assessed and then addressed with realistic contingency plans. One of Forrester's critical errors was that he'd had a weak risk plan that had unrealistic contingencies for the few real risks it addressed.

"I can't stress enough," Miller annunciated, "how important it is to make risk identification a continuous process and to make certain our contingency plans make sense." This wasn't news to anyone in the room. Each member of the group was smart or experienced enough to know that a risk plan was something that evolved over time, and that initial risk plans tended to go out the window once a program took on a life of its own. "Earl," Miller continued, "the reason I wanted you to take on this role is because you're extremely critical and brutally honest." Everyone chuckled because what Miller said was so obviously true.

Moving on, Miller explained that Parma Singh would be responsible for adoption management. "Your job is to get the users involved early on in the requirements process. Al and Jim can help you with some techniques, but I'm expecting you find creative ways to bring people in. Focus groups are a given. Workshops are highly recommended. But remember that while some of the folks you need to engage are on this campus, you're also dealing with folks in off shore call centers and satellite campuses. I think your challenge will be to help these folks feel plugged in, keep their anxiety level down, and find some way to give everyone a voice, even if we can't realistically respond to or satisfy absolutely everyone."

Miller went on to explain that one more person would be joining these team meetings before Labor Day – a liaison from the CFO's office who would manage budget issues. "If we're going to get the dollars we need, we have to make whoever this is feel like one of us, not like a spy from finance," Miller said plainly. "We're asking for more money, so we need to make whoever this is feel the love in here." Everyone chuckled quietly, except Campbell, who wondered aloud which bean counter old Lang might throw at them.

His jaded comment was interrupted as the door opened and Charlie Dowd stepped into the room. Everyone sat up a bit straighter as the new CIO walked in, but Charlie just smiled and said, "hey, at ease troops. I'm sorry I'm late. Unfortunately my 'other job' is a bit of a firestorm at the moment. Board members can be like hyenas if you let them…I know Miller is covering your roles and the state of the program. I just want to talk for a minute about the key changes we want to make and what our next steps are…if you don't mind Marc."

"Be my guest," Miller said and took a seat as Charlie squeezed his way to the head of the table. He flipped forward few a slides to one entitled "Major Changes" and showed the team a list that mostly summarized what had been discussed:

"I think this probably sums up the scope of what we need

Major Changes

- Engaging the business owners
- Establishing new requirements
- Working with the CFO on budget
- Re-structuring the PMO
- Bringing in a strong Systems Integrator
- Shifting to a "mall" architecture strategy
- Creating a new migration plan
- Making the vendors have some skin in the game
- Cancelling unnecessary projects and "shadow" organizations
- Re-invigorating the staff
- Reassessing program risks and putting continuous risk assessment in place
- Putting a "benefits realization" approach in place
- Promote Accountability
- Prepare the Infrastructure for Production
- Have a solid operating environment that will not fail as things start to move faster

MAJOR CHANGES

to do," Charlie said. "One thing that's not on this list though is follow-through. If all we do is build a new system and launch new products on it, we'll only achieve a cost increase and a new silo. The trick for us is to demonstrate to the Board that while the costs go up initially, we will reach a point of where we dramatically cut cost out of the business while increasing the top line because of the new services and sales processes we enable." Charlie scanned the faces in the room for acknowledgement as heads nodded in understanding.

"We'll need to develop a Benefits Realization model that shows the Board when the cost shift will actually happen, and then we need to hit all of those marks. We can't be overly ambitious – we'll do this in bite sized pieces - but we need to hit both sides. If this is all about cost savings, we're sunk. We've got less than eight weeks to figure this out and convince the Board we can predict the future. Understood?"

Heads nodded all around – even Campbell's - though Charlie could see that everyone had natural doubts and concerns. He'd be disappointed if they didn't.

"Here's another major point to think about," Charlie continued. "There needs to be a sense of urgency around this program. We have a bad impression to overcome that IT is a do-nothing organization. When everyone sweats, we sweat twice as hard. We also need to be brutally honest with each other. I don't want sugar coated reports from you guys…"

"No problem here," Campbell inserted. Charlie shot him a look that said, 'don't interrupt me right now.'

"As I was saying, I want the real story – the good, the bad, and the ugly. If I get flowers and fluff, you're going to have a problem with me. I'm the one who's out there selling this thing to the business every day, so I need the straight dirt. So starting next week we'll have a daily 7 a.m. status call so we all stay on the same page." Charlie didn't hear any groans, but he sensed them being internalized. "This hole is deep enough that we need to do this daily for now. The purpose of these calls is to stay in sync and address any issues. If you have gripes with each other, air them out on this call. If you think we're walking into a buzz saw, say so. But also, share some of the little victories. That will help keep all of us fresh. Some of these calls will last an hour or so. Some will be five minutes. But we'll have them every weekday. If we need to have them on weekends too, we will. If we can, we'll ultimately make them weekly. But not yet. Understood?"

Of course every one did. They didn't have much choice, but saw the wisdom in what Charlie was trying to do.

"I'll need to head to another meeting now but, Marc do you want to talk about the next couple of months?" Charlie suggested more than asked.

"Sure, let's look at the Discovery phase," Miller replied. Charlie waved and closed the door behind him quietly as he stepped out. "Our next two months are going to involve developing a working rhythm among this group. But what we'll mostly be focused on heading into this board assessment is a discovery phase. We need to get to the bottom of…" he hesitated, opening the door for Campbell.

"We've dubbed it Forrester's crevasse," Earl said, not bothering to hide his disdain for the former CIO. "Miller's our Sherpa," he quipped.

"Exactly," Miller said. "We've got to climb down into this thing, see what's there, and hope we can climb our way out." Everyone smiled and enjoyed the joke for a moment.

"To extend the metaphor," Miller continued, "you wouldn't be in this room if I didn't know you're an expert climber. We're going to be reading audit reports, project logs, and volumes of granular PMO reports that are lying around but were never really used for anything. We're going to interview the project managers that are still here. Parma, if you know some of the folks who've already left, let's get those folks in a room or on the phone and interview them too." She nodded and made a note for herself.

"Earl," Miller continued, "I need you to make sure everyone in this room knows where this program originally started, what happened while you were still involved, and what went wrong. At the end of this process, we need a clear and convincing story for how we'll fix things without repeating past mistakes. This will be tough because the discovery needs to happen in parallel with things like setting up the new PMO structure – that's you Jimmy – and all of the other responsibilities we discussed earlier. We're in for late nights and some heads banging against walls I think. But, if we do this right we should start to see some good progress pretty soon."

"Marc, if I may," Al Marcus interjected. Miller motioned to him to continue. "Where do you see me fitting into this discovery phase?"

"Fair question Al," Miller replied. "First, you'll help Earl and Jim with the go-forward plan, because your solution is going to be central to whatever the new architecture looks like. Second, I need you to bring back the real A-plus folks from Commapps as well as the most useful people you can find who understand how billing and customer care and support are done here. Then, anything you can do to help Parma get her feet on the ground," Parma and Al exchanged a quick glance and a smile, "I'm sure she would appreciate it."

"Makes sense," Al replied. "I've got some good people on the way already."

"Good to know," Miller said. With that, he shut down the projector. The team began to ask more of the questions they'd been scribbling down throughout the meeting, taking Charlie's point about "a sense of urgency" to heart.

Dos and Don'ts for Chapter 2	
DO:	**DON'T:**
Manage all aspects of the transformation – People, Process, and Technology.	Minimize the Program Management function or make it merely an extended project tracking role.
Establish an empowered program office with clear roles and responsibilities.	Fail to leverage useful tools that might be in place just because they were associated with a failed effort. They may have been misused or had nothing to do with the failure whatsoever.
Take the time and make the effort to assemble the best possible team and use every resource to provide them with incentives.	Fail to define deliverable schedules at a granular level to stay on top of progress and problems.
Understand the past failures and the reasons behind them.	Behave like a machine and forget that your people need to feel positive about where and for whom they work in order to succeed.
Define tight deliverables that represent discernible and incremental units of work	
Take care of your people and diffuse their tension.	

For more information on how EMC Consulting can assist you with your transformation visit: - **www.emc.com/services**

CHAPTER 3

Four weeks earlier, late in the first week of July, Al Marcus had been enjoying a cold drink in the lounge in his hotel in Singapore when his cell phone rang. It had been a long day full of meetings and mental arm wrestling and he answered the call begrudgingly. Swallowing the temptation to snap at the caller, along with a gulp of his iced tea, he realized he didn't recognize the number. He answered in his refined Oxford accent, "This is Al Marcus."

"Al, this is Lee Rosenberg. I'm glad I caught you."

Getting a surprise call from the CEO of the company was rarely a good sign. Al Marcus knew this lesson well, but was confused. In the span of a nanosecond he reviewed every possibility and couldn't figure one that made sense. His program was going better than could normally be expected. His deliverables were on time. The customer was happy and had put out several press releases regarding the capabilities their new billing solution was enabling for them.

"Lee, I must confess that I'm surprised to hear from you. To what do I owe the honor?"

"Well Al, I uh…I have a job for you."

"Yes?" Al knew this probably wasn't going somewhere good.

"Our role over at Unidigitel has been expanded."

Al had heard about this program and knew it wasn't going well. He'd thought a few months back that it might be a matter of time before he was called in to rescue it. But as time passed, he'd put it out of his mind and figured he might be out of the woods. He'd been wrong.

"I'm getting pressure from our board to make sure this program succeeds," Rosenberg told him. "Apparently, the program manager asked for you specifically, and when he was told you weren't available, one of our board members got a call from their CIO. So, I'll need you to pick someone from your team to replace you and get yourself to San Francisco as soon as possible."

Al choked down a snappy objection and said without his voice betraying his displeasure, "Lee, I've got 15 months in on this project. I'm in sight of the finish line. I'm not sure I'm prepared to walk away right now."

"Al, you've done a bang up job. So much so that the client is confident their folks can bring the project in from here with some of your top guys. I'm going to need you in San Francisco next week. We'll make it worth your while. Don't worry about that." Rosenberg implored him. "You need to go see Charlie Dowd and Marc Miller no later than July 15."

Al met Miller, Jim, and Charlie in the small conference room adjacent to Marc Miller's office. He needed to talk in detail with Miller and Dowd about how this new program was going to run. He'd been given briefs and notes several days before and understood the general architectural strategy, the shift in program management that was coming, and some of the history of the ailing program, but he needed some more tangible information from the two blokes in charge.

"As you probably know from my brief," Miller explained, "Forrester was arrogant, but he wasn't necessarily stupid. The business owners are all clamoring that he never engaged them, but from reading his notes it's pretty clear that in his mind he tried. It's just that he only dealt with the technical requirements. He really never looked at their processes, the undocumented workarounds, or tried to tackle any process re-engineering."

"Yes, I saw that. On paper, his architectural vision was creative. I'm not sure how far he got, or what went wrong – that's what I need to learn from you now – but I think I understand what he was trying to do."

Forrester had had an educated but impractical vision. When he took over as CIO, Unidigitel had a number of typical problems. Each of its major product areas – consumer voice; consumer data; wireless; and video – was managed from a distinct set of IT platforms, each with its own customer profiles; product catalogs;

ordering platforms; multiple billing systems; and service activation processes. Each product area was supported by a dedicated call center. There was also a self-help web portal that had been cobbled together. Customers could use a single log-in but all of the billing and ordering functionality was separated by product and no two screens looked or worked alike.

The result of having distinct operations platforms behind each service was significant redundancy, unnecessarily high operational costs, and no ability to provide a customer with centralized support across multiple services either via the web or from the call center. Customers were routed through convoluted support queues when trying to resolve billing disputes or troubleshoot service problems. Customer data was inconsistent across various databases because even changes to simple information, like a street address, would not always propagate across the platforms. Hold times were long, customers were frustrated, and Unidigitel struggled to bring enticing product bundles to market.

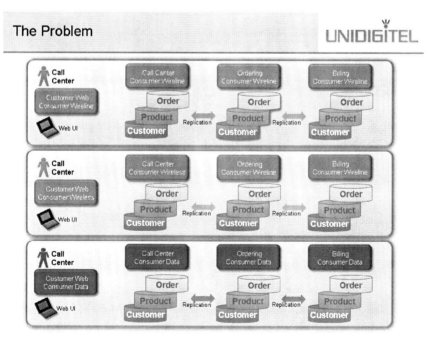

THE PROBLEM

Liz Fagan and the board had tasked Forrester with consolidating the underlying IT systems. Forrester was strong on theory, but inexperienced when it came to execution. The vision he painted for a simplified, streamlined and integrated architecture looked promising to the uninitiated as slideware. He proposed and designed an architecture that would collapse the disparate systems supporting the range of offerings. According to his plan, four key areas or quadrants would emerge.

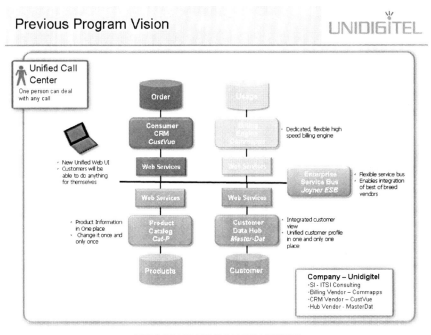

PREVIOUS PROGRAM VISION

One quadrant would handle ordering and CRM. All orders and order history for existing and new products would be migrated into or launched from a common order data repository that linked into a dedicated CRM application from one of Commapps' primary competitors. This CRM application would support a unified web portal that would handle ordering, billing, and support across all products. That web portal, albeit configured with different views and permissions, would serve as a common interface for care agents, retail store staff, and for online customer self-care.

Another quadrant would handle billing across all products from a dedicated, flexible, and high speed billing engine from Commapps. The platform would be supported with a centralized data store that would house all of the information regarding customers' service usage. The common billing platform and data store would make it easier to introduce price changes; would give contact center agents a common view of customers' billing and usage histories; and would give customers access to up-to-the-minute billing information through the new web portal.

A third quadrant would be built on a distinct product catalog solution from yet another vendor. Forrester's idea here was to centralize all product information so that any changes to products, or any new product introductions, would only have to occur in this one database and could then be shared across the rest of the architecture. This information would also feed into the web portal and contact centers and give agents and customers a common view of what services and new offers were available for ordering. It would also make new service creation simpler and allow for more complex and creative bundles to be introduced.

The fourth quadrant would be built on a customer data hub supplied by a fourth vendor company, MasterDat. The customer data hub would be accompanied by a centralized customer database to which all customer information would have to migrate. This platform would house unified profiles so that all information regarding a customer and its services would be accessible from a single point and would provide a common or integrated view. This view would feed into the CRM systems to support the contact center and would provide the basis for the customer-centric account views accessible through the new web portal.

The unifying element that would pull the four quadrants together was a new enterprise service bus, supplied by a fifth vendor that would enable the best of breed components to be integrated in a flexible way – rather than point to point. Ideally, the systems would be able to share and exchange information when necessary; common processes could be defined from a business perspective and flow freely across all of the platforms; and the unified web portal would have continuous access to accurate and up-to-date information from a customer-centric perspective.

From Forrester's point of view, this was an elegant architecture. What Al and everyone else quickly recognized, however, was that this approach would have been a program management nightmare. It involved far too many vendors and individual projects. Forrester compounded this by failing to focus on project coordination. Too much custom integration would be needed to get all of the systems to work in concert. Data conversion would prove extremely difficult, which made migration to centralized stores in a short period of time unrealistic. Add to that the fact that Forrester hadn't accounted well for business process re-engineering. This meant the streamlined characteristics of the new architecture wouldn't be leveraged and the unified web portal idea would flop. Further, a host of other technical problems could inevitably pop up that would torpedo the whole initiative. It was no wonder that it had imploded.

"One of the big problems I can see happened," Miller explained, "is that Forrester never looked at improving care or up-sales, cross-sales, promotions, marketing, or support. We're still running different call centers to support each service and customers are being bounced around because they don't know who to call for different problems. The agents aren't always sure where to send them. So, he aimed for this unified web portal, which was the right idea, but he never delivered it. Even if he had, he didn't work with the care organization to plan any sort of call center consolidation."

"I understand," Al said, "but the good news is that despite all of these existing products, and the fact that they are being delivered and supported through different organizations, we've seen this sort of thing plenty of times before," he said. "What will make this easier, based on what you gave me to read, is that you're not looking to customize the platform much. Leveraging our process flows and use cases - in my experience - is usually the best path. Reinventing the wheel, as you can imagine, is pretty painful."

"Right, but the real pressure here," Miller paused for just a moment, "is that we need to re-engage the business and be able to launch bundled products on this platform in a short period of time. What's playing against us is that we haven't quite gotten to the bottom yet of where the architecture stands now. That's where I need you to work with Earl during this discovery phase in the next six weeks. "

Al nodded in acknowledgement and scribbled down some notes as Miller continued.

"Charlie has to present a plan of attack to the board by September 1st. I'll need to get status from your people on what we can salvage, what we need to trash, what's been installed that works, what is and isn't integrated…And we need to support bundled products in year one from end to end on the new platform, which actually only gives us about ten months."

Al nodded, nearly frowned, and ran his fingers through his thinning hair as he considered Miller's words.

"The new architecture also needs to set the stage for year two – starting next June - where we start moving existing customers and some legacy products to it, collapsing some of those call centers, and de-commissioning some older systems. That's where this plan starts to pay off."

"I understand Marc," Al held up a hand to slow him down. "Until I get a real grasp of where things stand today and how they need to work, I won't be able to make much forward progress on the solution. I know that one major change from the original scope was that the CRM functionality was coming from another vendor. Do I understand that you now want to change that plan and have us install our CRM components as well. If so, are we developing completely new requirements for that?"

"Business requirements, yes. Some of the technical requirements, like most of the flows in the web portal, are probably salvageable to some extent," Charlie asserted. "Parma and I will be working with the business organizations and with Liz Fagan, our CEO, to address things like sales and customer experience. We need to define what we all really mean by customer-centricity, so it's not just a load of lip service. What I plan to make happen is that before requests hit your plate, we'll handle as much of the prioritization and push back as possible with the business and users to make sure you can stay focused. But, I won't lie to you, sometimes for the sake of diplomacy you'll end up being the bad guy…" Charlie let his comment hang and Al jumped on it.

"Yes, and of course. Not to worry. I'm happy to play the villain if that's what it takes. If you asked my ex-wife, she would tell you I am well suited to it."

"Alright then Al," Miller said through a half-snort, "you'll need to get your team up to speed, sync up with Earl, and kick off the discovery process as fast as possible."

Al Marcus had to pull his team together from in-house staff, Commapps people who were already on site, and key 'A' talents he trusted and could shake loose from other projects. He held weekly status meetings to keep his team in sync and to address any issues that emerged during the discovery phase. In the third of these meetings, he decided to change gears. At this point his team understood the architectures' status and the general changes they had to make to it. Al, however, wanted to ensure that his team felt free to voice their concerns about these changes and give them confidence that he could lead them through the inevitable pitfalls.

"Okay everyone, settle down," Marcus said to kick off the meeting. He was glad to hear collegial banter regarding the project. Ultimately, his people needed to come to a consensus and trust each other. He took the pointed but friendly debates as a sign they were engaged. "To start things off...I know you all have concerns. We've done well in understanding what's gone wrong with this program in the past and where we stand now. Today I want to make sure we address issues that some of you raised with me about our next steps. As we come out of this discovery effort, we need to factor these issues into the recommendations we'll make in just a few weeks. It might seem a bit childish, but I'm going to go around the room and ask you to help me come up with a list."

Various members of the team, senior and junior, voiced their concerns – only a few of them redundant – and Al Marcus wrote a succinct list on the whiteboard with a black dry-erase pen. The list read:

Implementation Concerns
- Business Buy-in
- Scope and Requirements Creep
- Customization Issues
- Impact of Business Process Definition
- User Training and Adoption

"Let's tackle each of these items one by one now," Marcus continued. "Each one of these has the potential to become a festering problem, so let's make sure we all understand what processes we need to establish and steps we need to take to deal with them."

Dealing with creeping scope and changing requirements was an issue for any program. At this point, the requirements for the program were being completely reassessed and the scope scaled back. That, however, did not mean that as the program progressed the scope would not or could not spiral out of control again.

"We'll be working with Charlie Dowd and Parma Singh directly on the business requirements. They've promised to prioritize what they derive from the business owners and users. It will be up to us to recommend the best way to meet these requirements based on what we know about our software and the assets we have off the shelf. We also need to push back against anything that's unrealistic or can derail our schedule. I don't think we'll win every battle, but Charlie expects us to hold our ground. Gail, I'll ask you to stay in touch with Parma to stay ahead of any requirements changes that might be thrown at us from the user community."

Gail Sawyer nodded in acknowledgement and said, "Al, let's make sure we also cover the technical requirements problem we had before. One of the major problems we all saw develop was that any time someone from this team, or some other IT team, came up with a, let's say, *creative* new idea, Forrester fell in love with it and forced it into the schedule. That's a big reason why so much time was wasted in the past year."

"Good point Gail. Let me address this directly." Marcus replied. "We're locking down the scope of the technical requirements as of September 15th. The business folks need to understand that, but also need visibility into how we'll address important new requirements and changes in subsequent versions. Let's make sure they understand that failure to lock down the requirements was a major reason this program failed on the first go round." Heads nodded in acknowledgement. Gail Sawyer raised a hand.

"Go ahead Gail," Marcus said gesturing toward her.

"I just want to reiterate for everyone, because we haven't discussed this for a few weeks that Al and Jim Taylor have to approve all requirements and change requests as a matter of practice anyway. We have a lot of back up here," she said.

"That's right," Marcus continued. "Remember also that we're not bringing in any add-on components as was the case previously. If we run into a conflict with the business owners as a result, the issue would escalate to Marc Miller who could then take it to Charlie Dowd and ultimately to the steering committee. That process alone would likely slow things down long enough to take the shine off any half-baked ideas."

Several of the team members smiled, and others chuckled quietly at this comment.

"The next item I want to dig into is the customization issue," Al said. "Right now, I do not have a clear picture of how much our solution has been altered, what would be involved in restoring it to a more standard state, or what customization might become necessary based on the new business requirements. The latter we won't know until, again, we have results from Charlie and Parma. Who can give me a status on where the solution stands now from this perspective?"

Near the end of the table, one of the junior members of the team apprehensively raised a hand. "Mr. Marcus, I might have some insight here."

"Go ahead Ritesh. Speak up."

Ritesh Dhar was only 25, but the other folks in the room didn't object when he volunteered to answer the question. A bit shy and inexperienced in this situation, everyone at least recognized his technical talents and his familiarity with the billing solution.

"Well Mr. Marcus, fortunately the data models have been left intact, which makes things a bit easier. But we had to custom build many of the input-output processes and wrap the standard APIs to accommodate the best-of-breed integration. This required us to change the way we handled many standard processes within the solution."

"Ritesh, can you provide me with a written summary of what's been changed and whether it can be undone or reused. Understand that we'll need to make a decision quickly whether or not to start again from scratch."

"Yes Mr. Marcus. I already have a spreadsheet that keeps track of many of these changes. I don't think we'll have to start over again entirely, but I do think that re-use of what's been written, given the architectural changes, will be very limited."

"Many thanks Ritesh, and well done." Dhar nearly smiled and sat up just a bit straighter in his chair in response to this bit of praise from his manager.

The solution team's dependence on business re-alignment was clear to everyone in the room. Marcus didn't feel the need to reiterate in detail what had already been noted numerous times. Instead he said, "I think everyone can see that we're counting on the CIO to bring the business folks to the table and that he's in the process of doing that now. Let's assume that in the next week or so we'll begin to hold some workshops ourselves to figure out how best to deal with things like orders, support, and customer care flows."

"That doesn't mean, however," Al continued, "that we can't begin to install the application in the lab and get the fundamental pieces of those connectors up and running. For now, let's focus on the items we've addressed in this meeting that we can affect immediately. We'll table training and user adoption until a later time, when Parma is ready to work with us there. But let's make sure we address that early in our workshops and be precise with our documentation. User adoption will ultimately drive the success or failure of this project. We want to make sure we have a head start on field guides and training manuals when Parma does come calling for them."

What Marcus did not say was that under terms of Commapp's expanded contract, payments would not be made unless and until the user's cut over to the new system and embraced it. How Miller had worked that into the arrangement he wasn't sure, but he knew it was his responsibility if, in the end, the new solution wasn't adopted wholly.

By mid-August, after six weeks of combing through audit reports, interviewing people who'd worked under Forrester, and examining the software components Al Marcus' team was working on, Earl Campbell believed he had an accurate and detailed view of the architectures current state. Al's team members from Commapps had been instrumental in developing this view. They all now sat in a cramped conference room to present the total results of their findings to Charlie Dowd and Marc Miller and to propose a new architecture that could fix what had gone terribly wrong.

The members of Al's team consisted largely of the folks who'd been working on the Unidigitel project for Commapps. It also included two project managers from Unidigitel's IT staff who Forrester had assigned to help implement the new billing platform and integrate it with the CRM, product catalog and customer data hub components.

As the discovery phase began, the folks from Commapps were mostly B-teamers who'd been moved to the program nearly eight months into Forrester's debacle. They were knowledgeable and would prove useful going forward, but Al had to reach out to the A-teamers who'd been assigned to the project originally to see what more he could learn. He also had continued to nudge the home office to re-assign some of his top folks back onto his project team as they rolled off the engagement in Singapore, and a few of those he'd wanted were in the room now.

Earl Campbell, of course, was prepared to kick off the meeting with a blunt evaluation of what Forrester had tried to do, why it was bound to fail, and how he, Miller, Marcus and several of the A-team players figured it needed to change.

"The bottom line," Campbell began, "is that Bradley fell in love with the idea that he could integrate anything to anything and it steered everything he wanted to do. He thought he could build his ideal architecture by customizing a whole slew of off-the-shelf software and integrate it through an enterprise bus. He wanted to create several centralized data stores to handle orders, usage, products and customers. He thought this would let the business guys create all the new services, product offerings, marketing campaigns, and billing schemes they wanted."

"But in doing so he tried to boil the ocean..." Marcus added.

"Exactly," Campbell continued, "He figured that if the apps he brought in couldn't handle the functionality he wanted, he'd have some of the folks in this room, and a bunch of people who ultimately left, write code. He spent most of his time and money trying to wire all of this stuff together. He was trying to get billing, CRM and provisioning up and running all at once. At the same time he wanted to migrate all of the customer data. He figured that he'd pull this all off in a year and then year two would be a clean-up exercise where he could just keep moving products and any stragglers over to the new system."

"What about the unified contact center interfaces he was building?" Dowd asked to try and keep Campbell on point.

"Well, his slideware showed a unified call center, and he cobbled together a web interface, but he didn't try to re-engineer any of the processes to support any consolidation."

"So we don't have a good idea of how the existing processes work now?" Dowd asked. "Before I go back to the business owners, you need to give me an idea of how things run now and what they might need to look like to work with the new solution."

"Charlie, you realize that means you'll need to sell the sales and product guys on the idea that they need to change what they're doing. I mean, Forrester could have done a better job of working with them, but that doesn't mean they're easy to work with. I know those guys, and they're a bunch of cry babies," Campbell scoffed.

"Take it easy Earl," Dowd retorted. "That's why I'm taking that on myself."

"Alright, fair enough…"

"Earl," Al Marcus interjected, "why don't we get back to the status of the architecture and go through it step by step for Charlie and Miller." He appreciated Campbell's enthusiasm, but could see a rant coming on.

"Okay, okay. Here's what it looks like now." Campbell hit a button on his laptop and a slide representing the current state of Forrester's largely failed program appeared on the projection screen at one end of the room.

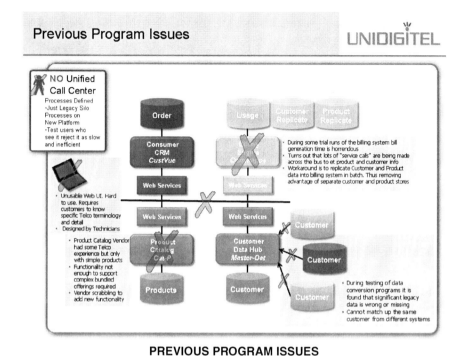

PREVIOUS PROGRAM ISSUES

"Well Earl, that's a disappointing number of red Xs you've got there," Miller egged him on and Dowd shot him a look in reply. Miller shrugged and smirked.

"Yeah, well let me explain. Forrester didn't engage the business, like we said, so he didn't manage to define any unified call center processes. The genius went to the trouble of designing a unified architecture to support a common call center, but then he planned to move the old processes to the new platforms. So, we've had to rework those business requirements entirely."

"Makes sense," Charlie said. "And from what I've seen that the alpha version of the web interface he built was that it's not going to be very useful to us. It's not intuitive."

"That's right. That web-based user interface is basically unusable. A customer needs a seminar in telco-speak to figure it out and there's really no logical or intuitive flow to it. It's a do-over for sure. That's a critical piece to making this whole thing fly with the users."

"Okay. No surprises so far," Miller said. "Tell us the story about this X over the product catalog."

"Well, you'll love this one," Campbell continued. "The vendor Forrester picked to supply the product catalog claimed to have all kinds of telco experience, but the templates they had could only handle simple products. It wasn't going to support anything like a personalized bundle or services that span multiple networks. They started hammering away at it; adding new functionality, customizing it…it's a real mess."

"But the streamlined approach you guys have been talking about should eliminate that anyway, right?" asked Miller.

"Yeah, but you're jumping ahead," Campbell retorted. "If you look over here at the billing engine," he pointed to the upper right hand corner of the slide, "obviously we want to keep Al's system in place, but Forrester created a bunch of problems around it that we need to deal with. First, his decision to go with a separate CRM component caused all kinds of issues."

"I could have predicted this," Marcus interjected. "I've seen it before. You can't translate orders coming out of that CRM system into our billing solution very well."

"Right," Campbell continued. "Neither system looks at anything the same way. You have different data formats where, for example, they don't even store dates or customers' names in the same way. The semantics are all screwed up too. You have a field for unit cost, but the unit in the CRM system is a bundle. In the billing system a unit is just one element of a bundle. And then the definitions are all different. They don't define products or equipment the same way. Like, the CRM system calls for a DSL modem, but the billing system is more specific and it wants to know whether it's a Motorola ADSL modem or a Cisco VDSL modem."

"So," Miller said, "I'll assume he wrote a load of code, that you can't maintain, to translate the orders from the CRM system and force them into the billing platform."

"Exactly…but it gets better."

Miller and Dowd exchanged a glance as Campbell continued.

"When they started trial runs on the new billing system in the lab, the bill generation time was just horrendous. It turns out that Bradley's beautiful architecture had to make all kinds of service calls across the enterprise bus to get product and customer info. So he invented a workaround that basically nullified his whole centralized database approach."

"Which was…? Dowd asked.

Marcus picked up where Campbell left off saying, "This is something I've also seen before. He decided to replicate the customer and product data into the billing system's database in batch form. So, he not only negated the purpose of having separate, centralized databases, but also created a synchronization problem. The billing system performance might have improved, but it was ultimately going to spit out the wrong information and be a bear to maintain."

"Okay," Miller said. "So, that explains the Xs over the billing engine and the bus. What about this one on the bottom right, over by the customer databases."

"This is where things really blew up in his face. We have a lot of customer data out there. It's spread across more databases than what you see on this slide, and it's in about eight different formats, or worse. They got the customer data hub up and running, but when they started testing the data for conversion they hit a wall."

"Who is they?" Dowd asked, a bit hot under the collar. "Was anyone in this room involved in that effort?"

One of the junior members of the team timidly raised a hand at the end of the table.

"Remind me of your name again?" Charlie asked, gesturing toward the young man.

"I am Ritesh Dhar, Mr. Dowd," he said with a slight Indian accent. "I worked for a bit on the customer data hub integration. I was part of a three person team. The two others have left the company. We told Mr. Forrester that centralizing this customer information was going to be problematic, but he did not want to listen. He insisted that we install the data hub and begin connecting it with the enterprise service bus, so we did. But not one of us was surprised when we began to test the data and had problems."

"Thank you Ritesh. Earl, sum up the problems for me."

"Well Charlie, as you probably can guess, there was all kinds of legacy data that was missing, or just wrong. It all needed to be scrubbed. And even if they managed to scrub it all, they couldn't match customers up from different systems. So, centralizing all of this customer data was going to be – and is going to be – a real challenge. I'd say we're going to need some extra hands on deck to handle this one. Ideally, that's a group with some data transformation tools and experience that we don't have in-house or can't spare and probably some third party data suppliers too."

"Okay, Earl, and thank you," Miller followed on. "So, Charlie, you can see that we've got a clear picture now of the status of this thing. We also have a plan cooking for how we can fix it, which you asked to see today. Al?"

"Before we get into that," Charlie interjected, "I think we need to recognize that some of the data we're touching, the product data in particular, needs to be consolidated and cleansed, in addition to the customer data. I know, for example, that Liz wants us to simplify the wireless rate plans and keep the bundle pricing simple. But we can't force these changes on anyone. We need to work with people in marketing and sales in the different product groups on what the new offerings will look like. I'm working on finding the right representative from the business to help us build a bridge there. Liz, obviously, will champion us too, but I'll have to handle this diplomatically. So we need to stay flexible for now. Understood?" Miller and Campbell shrugged and nodded. "Good. Go ahead Al."

"Certainly," Marcus said. "The good news is that we're going to eliminate most of the custom-code work and the performance issues because we're going to jettison the old CRM component and use the pre-integrated Commapps solution for that. My team knows how to bring those pieces together and what the pitfalls are. Several of us just went through a similar process in Singapore," Al nodded toward several members of his 'A' team.

"We're also prepared to re-engineer the support processes so we can achieve a unified call center model," he continued. "We host most of the customer and product data on our platform, along with the billing information. There will still be some risk there in migration, and surely there will be requests from the business we'll have to jigger things to support, but it should all be more contained with our new approach. In other words Charlie, we can in fact be somewhat flexible for you as the business folks make their decisions."

Marcus nodded at Campbell who clicked his mouse and brought a new slide into focus on the projection screen.

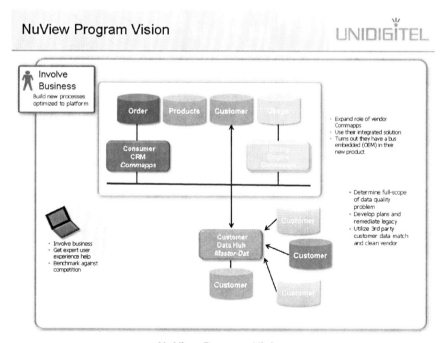

NuView Program Vision

"Now, if I can direct your attention to this slide, I'll explain our ideas for moving forward," Marcus continued. "The reason you brought me here was that Miller decided, and rightly in my opinion, that our solution could become the anchor point for a revised and streamlined architecture. There are several pieces that have been implemented, or that are partially implemented, that we are going to sever. As I said, we're first going to replace the incompatible CRM component with our own system and take advantage of the pre-integration there. This should eliminate the custom code work and take some performance concerns out of the picture."

"How pre-integrated is that pre-integrated CRM piece?" Dowd asked directly.

"That's a good question," Marcus replied. I can say from experience that it should give us about 80 percent of what we need out of the box. We won't run into the kinds of data transformation and order incompatibility problems we had before, so the 20 percent that's remaining will depend largely on how the processes for customer care and product support are defined. And of course, on how well the data scrubbing and migration goes. I'd say that's a line item for the risk plan though."

"Noted," said Dowd, "which means two things. First, I'll need to stay in touch with you about what the business owners are saying and you'll need to help me sell them on leveraging your solution assets. Also, your team will have to work with Jim and Earl to stay on top of the data issues and how that impacts the rest of the schedule."

"I agree," Marcus replied, "but in my experience, on the business requirements, there is enough flexibility that you should not be overly limited. I can show them use cases from some of the best in the world that I should think will be exciting for them. Further, the pre-integration is largely based on a bus that is embedded in our product – an OEM component. That will replace the ESB that created the performance problems. This will make the CRM integration easier, as we said, but it will also allow us to future-proof the architecture a bit. It should also help us to salvage much of the work that's already been done on the customer data hub. Does that make sense?"

"Yes, but explain it for everyone anyway," Dowd said.

"Right. The product catalog project, which is only partially completed, will cease. It will be replaced by the product catalog that is part of our billing solution and which works with our CRM component. The same can be said of our ordering database and our billing or usage database. All of these components are native to our solution. So again, we'll benefit from independent and centralized data stores but we will cut down significantly on the effort to integrate them and perform data transformation across the bus. In concept, we'll do what Forrester had planned, but with a much easier and better integrated means of executing it."

"Okay, but that leaves the whole customer data hub issue. How are we dealing with that?"

"Well, as you can see, we have a customer data store and format that is native to our system that we'd like to leverage. But we also have this customer data hub product that is implemented and the beginnings of a plan to migrate the disparate customer data stores to it. What Miller and I have discussed is that one of the projects we'll assign to ITSI is to determine the full scope of our data quality problem, develop a plan for scrubbing that data, and remediate the legacy data stores. We believe we can use a 3rd party customer data provider to match and clean much of the data, which should help us move a bit faster. In the meantime, we will launch our bundles and migrate only new customers – customers that take up any new offers or promotions - on the new platform in year one, with a goal of migrating all customers to the centralized store beginning in year two. The customer data hub that is already installed will provide a centralized access point into the disparate customer databases, really a federated approach, that we can use to support our unified call center and web portal processes in the interim."

"Which is where I come in," Charlie said.

"Precisely. There are two areas where we need input from the business owners and users – in the unified contact center, and on the web portal. We'd like to build new care and support processes that are optimized to our platform. We'll do our best to accommodate their vision, but ultimately, if we want to make this happen smoothly, it will be easier for them to adopt some of our best practices and use cases. I will help you sell them on that Charlie, as we said earlier."

"And what about the web portal?"

"This is another area where ITSI should help us out," Miller suggested. "We want to involve the business and user groups in creating the look, feel and flow of the portals, but we want to leverage the best user experience people from ITSI to make sure it's something that works for our customers too. We'll also ask them to benchmark our portal against our competitors and some leaders from other industries so we can roll something out that works well, is easy to use, and ideally is ahead of our direct competition."

"So, you know my next question," Charlie said. "When can we expect this re-architecture to be completed and how long is it going to take? Or put another way – can you have this done and have our new products up and running on it by the time we need to deliver this and some tangible results to the Board next summer?"

"We think so, but…" Earl Campbell's pregnant pause keep the room silent for a few seconds that felt like minutes, "…this all depends on the business folks getting on board with what we're trying to do here; on the systems integrators delivering some pieces on time; on the call center folks adopting the new systems and processes pretty smoothly; and on some new development work that the Commapps' people are doing on their CRM solution. My job is to assess the risks and, in my opinion, these are the dependencies we need to have contingency plans to deal with. I think we can overcome them

Charlie, and deliver something that the board will be happy with. Experience tells me though that it'll probably look a bit different than what we're shooting for today. And we just added another risk item that we need to assess more completely – the data."

"Fair enough Earl," Charlie said. "Just remember what I've said all along though. Everyone in this room is accountable for making commitments and sticking to them. I know things will change along the way, but you need to communicate – that's why I want the program team on those 7 a.m. calls. There are no excuses. Legitimate issues are things I can live with, but if I start seeing things going from green to red, don't be surprised if I jump on you for it. That said, I have the utmost confidence that we have the right people on this job and that we'll all deliver – starting with me. I'll bring the business around, and you'll all give me the tools I need to win them over."

Dos and Don'ts for Chapter 3	
DO:	**DON'T:**
Have a well defined process to manage requirements.	Assume because it works for somebody else it will work for you. Scalability has dimensions of people and process as well as throughput.
All participants should be fully aware of deadlines and the impact of changes.	Over customize commercial software. It then simply becomes customized software.
Test, evaluate and gradually increase the utilization of new technology based on proven scalability.	Leave preparation and operational testing of a production grade environment until the last minute
Balance the way an organization wants to work with the way a packaged application wants to work or has been proven to work best.	Overlook business requirements and opportunity to improve process by focusing solely on technical requirements.
Have a plan that contains scope and has business sign-off.	Assume that what is the "latest and greatest" today still will be two years down the road.
Remember that time erodes functionality.	Overlook the fact that the Board and Executive team have to be involved throughout.
Engage the Board and Executives to win and maintain their buy-in.	Be afraid to make tough decisions when massive changes are needed to stop bleeding cash and recover .

For more information on how EMC Consulting can assist you with your transformation visit: - **www.emc.com/services**

CHAPTER 4

At 6:59 a.m. on Monday morning, Charlie Dowd dialed into the conference bridge to kick off the daily status call with the program team. His choice to take on re-aligning the massive IT program with the business owners' needs meant that he was central to the program and would have to roll up his sleeves and do some hard work. Too often he'd encountered managers he considered empty suits. They failed to earn loyalty, enforce accountability, and create a sense of real urgency. These were, in his opinion, critical to a program's success. So here he sat, alone at a booth in a local pancake house with a cup of coffee, a half eaten plate of bacon and eggs, a wrinkled copy of Newsweek, and his cell phone.

"There are *three* parties in conference," the recorded voice told him after he entered the pass code.

"Hi, this is Marc, who just joined the call?"

"It's me, Charlie. Good morning Marc. You're early for once."

"Yeah, my daughter was up at 6 with a stomach ache."

As the two chatted a bit aimlessly in the bleary eyed morning several tones sounded to signal the arrival of others on the bridge. Parma Singh and Jim Taylor each said "good morning" and waited for Charlie or Miller to start the discussion.

"Who are we still waiting for?" Miller asked to no one in particular.

"Earl's here with me on speaker, Marc. We've been going over the new architecture since about 6," Jim Taylor said.

Good, Charlie thought to himself. They're getting the urgency message.

"Have you guys seen or heard from Al yet?" Miller asked Jim.

"I'm on Marc. Just had you on mute. We can get started."

"Good morning Al," Charlie said. "Let's get moving. Our meeting a few days back about the new architecture was productive. I've begun to reach out to some of the folks I need to wrangle to drive the business alignment effort. Jim, are you comfortable with the mechanics of this thing and where your program management office needs to go?"

"Well," Taylor replied, "Earl sent me the slides over the weekend. He and I have been working our way through things for about the last hour. So, I'm getting there as far as the architectural details go. Most of it is pretty logical, though I do share a few concerns with Earl about the timing and some of the dependencies. That said, my real next step is getting the folks from ITSI Consulting spooled up on what they need to do, and I've already got an issue log that's longer than…it's long. Sorry. Anyway, I'd say that my biggest concern at the moment, in regards to the architecture, is getting the hardware we need. Right now, it looks like it'll take about three months based on how the procurement and P.O. processes seem to work. Obviously we're going to need to do something about that."

"Okay," Charlie responded. "What's the story with the issue log? Are we talking about new items, or just a lot of old items that haven't been dealt with?"

"It's a bit of both," Taylor said. "It's like a knot we have to untie. There's really no sort of a graduated system for tracking issues here. So, things have tended to go from green to red pretty quickly. We need to sort out which are priorities, which are irrelevant because of the architecture and project changes, and which we can put on the back burner for now. As we do that, though I need to get everyone on board with a better way to track and report status and create a few different escalation chains. There are things here that I want the project managers to deal with themselves, but still report status up to the PMO. Everything used to go right to Forrester, so some of the folks at the lower levels are used to either running alone until an issue went red,"

"…because they didn't want to deal with Bradley!" Campbell commented in the background.

"Or," Taylor continued, "in the reverse they wouldn't really want to take accountability so they just red lighted things, sent them up the chain, and waited for orders."

"Okay Jim," Charlie interrupted. "I hear you. You and Marc need to work on putting those processes in place and educating the project managers on how you want them to operate. You need to sort out and prioritize those issue logs too. The hardware issue probably falls a bit into my domain, so let me address that. I have a meeting later today with Lang Willis, the CFO. I'm going to ask him for a liaison from his office to join our group. I want to make sure finance is involved and backing us up, so hopefully we can deal with the P.O. and budget issue there. But, I've been thinking that I don't really want you guys worried about scrounging for gear or tools when you have bigger issues to deal with. We should identify someone we can add to this group to handle the engine room, so to speak…someone who knows how to deal with IT operations. We need a battle tested veteran type who can bring some order to the data centers and the network, who can deal with production issues, keep the operation humming, and who knows how to skirt some of the bureaucracy and scrounge for resources. I'll take suggestions if anyone has them."

There was silence on the line as everyone waited for someone to answer. Not surprisingly, that someone was Earl Campbell.

"I would have recommended Walt Brown about 6 months ago, but the nut decided he wanted to be a hot dog eating champion or something, gained about 75 pounds and ended up in the hospital on disability. So, he's out. I'll try to think of someone else, but a lot of those veteran folks left the company. And, while we're on that subject, one of the issues I want to mention is that we're going to have a tough time getting the right subject matter experts at the project level. Some of the best people have already left, so we're either going to need to get them back or rely on some second and third stringers to get things back on track."

"Fair enough Earl. We can take that discussion offline. I think we're all somewhat aware of that, but we'll need to sit down and take a closer look at who we have, who we don't, what ITSI can bring us, and whether we're overlooking anyone. So, that said, Parma, what's happening in your world?'

"Well sir," Parma said, "as you know, you and I are scheduled this week to meet with several of the business owners so we can begin to work with them on where we are trying to steer the program," Parma said with her accent that combined her roots in Mumbai with her British education.

"I've had some informal meetings with a few of them," she continued, "and I have an idea of who will be helpful, who will be resistant, and who will be completely insincere. My biggest concerns are the gentlemen who head up sales for wireless and video. The video team is accustomed to working on its own and is extremely wary of having their products and their numbers tied into other product lines as we bundle more. The man who leads wireless sales is altogether difficult. He is temperamental and autocratic with his people. He typically gets good results, which is why he is here, but he is not accustomed to cooperating and is protective of his domain. I need to get past him in order to engage the retail store users who are almost entirely in the wireless group."

"Well, I'll tell you what Parma. I will back you up, and if we ultimately need to take this issue up to the steering committee, we'll do that. But in the meantime, it's up to you to try to bring him around. Understood?"

"Yes sir. I will do my best," Singh said, a bit resignedly.

"Okay folks, unless there are any other issues to bring up, let's just talk quickly about what needs to happen this week and I'll let you get your days started…or continued."

As Charlie closed his cell phone and put it back on the table, he took a swig of his coffee and realized it had gone cold. It was late August and the air conditioning duct was blasting cold air right at him. He began to thumb through his copy of Newsweek when a hint of a shadow blocked his light. He looked up, expecting to see the waitress stepping up to refill his cup, but instead saw a woman's face he didn't recognize.

She was a woman in her mid-forties, with short, dark brown hair, no make-up, and wire rimmed bifocals that made her smallish eyes look almost squinted. No slave to the gym, she had a fleshy look about her, but an intensity that anyone who encountered her would sense immediately.

"Charlie Dowd, right?"

"That's right. What can I do for you?"

"Mr. Dowd, my name's Pat Morton. I saw your post on the Intranet bulletin board where you said you were here some-times in the early mornings and welcomed visitors. I've heard a little bit about what you're trying to do, but I need to be frank with you. Most of it probably isn't going to work. I figured if you're the kind of guy who eats breakfast in a place like this, you might not be some stuffed shirt. You might be willing to hear what someone like me has to say."

Charlie was fazed only momentarily by Pat Morton's directness, but as he studied her, he arrived at the conclusion that speaking to this woman for a few minutes was the sort of reason he was frequenting this little dive of a breakfast joint to begin with. "Have a seat. Can I get you some coffee or some-thing?"

"No, I don't drink the stuff. I had a bite to eat at the counter, so I'm fine."

"Okay. Pat, you'll have to forgive the fact that I don't have any idea of who you are. Obviously you work for Unidigitel but I don't know much more than that."

"I work in the research library, which basically means no one will bother to fire me, but I'm not exactly on what they call the fast track. I used to work in the IT organization. I had my own development group. But, uh, well what's-his-face didn't really like people who dealt in reality. I grew tired of dealing with him and got myself transferred to the library. I've been col-lecting paychecks and reading industry journals for the last six months."

"I take it you're not happy about that."

"Well, it beat working for wonder boy, but I suspect I can contribute more to the company than I am now. I thought about leaving, but then Bradley was canned. I'll get my pension in a few years, so I stuck around. I've been following your moves. Your guy Miller seems like a pretty good kid. I've heard him talking in the cafeteria from time to time. Smart guy. A little frenetic, but it's pretty well directed. But, uh, this plan you have going…It looks okay on paper, but you've got some issues."

Charlie was waiting for the punch line and said, "Why don't you enlighten me to your perspective."

"Gladly," she said without a hint of emotion. "First of all, you need someone who can crack the whip on your project teams. You've got all of these outsiders, and they're good at what they do, but most of the project managers and staff aren't really going to hop for them when it comes down to it. Campbell was a good choice, but he's an architect. He draws good pictures and tells it like it is, but he's not exactly a motivator. You haven't dealt with what'll happen when you try to get the users pulled in. Plus, you've got supply chain issues that no one on your team knows how to deal with. You need hardware that you're not going to get by filing paperwork and waiting for a P.O. to come through."

"We're you listening to our call?" Charlie asked, surprised by her intimate knowledge of his team's issues.

"I heard some of what you said, from over there. But let's say I have my sources. You don't really think I spend all of my time in the library do you?"

"I guess not." Charlie wondered who was leaking the information, but wasn't particularly concerned about it either. "Alright Pat, let me throw this at you. You obviously understand the problems. Can you offer us any useful solutions to them?"

"Probably," she said matter-of-factly.

"I'm looking for a straw boss for our IT Operations. Someone seasoned, talented, and frank. I don't need a complainer. I need someone who'd rather put out fires than start them. I'd consider you for this position, but I'd need to learn more about you…"

"I'm free now," she interrupted.

"Okay. But I'd also need you to meet with Marc Miller and Jim Taylor, get to know them. If they think you're right for this job, I'd give you a shot at it. Would that interest you?"

"It might. What's your definition of 'straw boss'?"

"The straw boss needs to prepare the IT infrastructure for this solution, including the network, the data center, product support, and end-user support. You'd have to be on call 24 hours a day, every day and wear a beeper. You'd have to be able to recognize when things look…too loose. Understand?"

"Yes."

"Good. The straw boss is also the final point of push-back on all infrastructure changes. You'd have to keep the ship running tightly and also keep me out of trouble."

"So I'd report to you?" she asked.

"Well, technically speaking you'd report to Marc Miller. But you'd have open lines of communication to me. We'd have to stay in sync, especially while I'm dealing with requests from the business owners."

"Right...Other than the supply chain stuff, what would you have me do during the development phases, pre-production?"

Charlie nodded slowly. "Let's spend a little time this morning talking about that. I've got about an hour before I need to be anywhere, and we can follow up from here."

Charlie and Pat spent the better part of the next hour exchanging war stories and talking about the history of Unidigitel's IT operations. Much of it he'd heard before, if not quite with Morton's particularly incisive point of view. What he learned was that she was a graduate of Northeastern University who got her start in IT working part time loading tapes in a data center while still a student. She'd come up through the ranks and was a battle tested operator. She knew the business inside and out, but had passed on several promotions that would have taken her out of operations. As a result, she was never given quite as much credit as she might have deserved. She believed she was respected, if not feared, more than she was necessarily liked. She'd worked hard over the years to build a reputation with various business owners as someone who could see nonsense coming from a mile away.

"She might be useful to us…" Charlie thought to himself as they said goodbye and went their separate ways. He put their conversation in the back of his mind, made a mental note to make sure she connected with Miller and Jim Taylor. He was then off to prepare for several upcoming meetings he had that week with groups of business and functional owners and with members of the executive steering committee he was assembling.

Charlie's first official meeting of the day was a project update where he was to meet with several senior functional owners he'd involved in the program's requirements discussions. In his first couple of weeks with Unidigitel, nearly three months earlier, Charlie had called a requirements review meeting to assess its status. While a few project managers and plenty of low level developers and architects attended, there wasn't a senior manager anywhere in the vicinity. That was the day he realized the true depth of the problems he'd have to solve. The program had acquired a nasty taint. No one in a position of responsibility wanted to be associated with it. Doubt began to creep into the far corners of his mind.

But through several months of selling, cajoling, and convincing, Charlie had pulled a number of senior managers from billing, customer care, sales, and product management into a series of workshops. Without their support and cooperation it would be extremely difficult to align the program's requirements with their needs and the numbers they had to make. The program could not operate in isolation anymore. It had to be a collaborative effort.

Charlie had to win support from a group of people who were confident, if not stubborn, and who had little reason to believe that anyone, no matter their track record, could set this program straight. During Charlie's workshops, they began to open up about how they wanted to improve their operations.

They were just beginning to understand how they'd affect each other in a simplified IT and operations environment that pulled their products and functional areas together.

"I want to be completely candid with you all," Charlie told the group after a few minutes of general chatter during one such workshop. "I think most of you are beginning to see that there are distinct benefits this program might deliver. I won't blow smoke at you about what looks good on paper. There are risks here. Some of them we've already identified. Others are going to pop up as we move forward. If we communicate, we'll stay ahead of those risks and deal with them." Heads began to nod around the room. Charlie continued.

"If we don't maintain transparency, there will be the kind of drama and conspiracy that derailed this program in the first place." No one was sold yet, but they all agreed the program was a mess because Forrester promised massive benefits and didn't deliver. He failed to communicate any sort of progress during his fateful year in command and had lost the confidence of the managers now involved in Charlie's workshops.

"Now," Charlie said, "I've told the folks on my team that we need to communicate when things are going wrong. I always say that bad news doesn't improve with age. I hope you'll all embrace that idea too." In laying this on the table, Charlie was calculating that if he couldn't convince these folks to engage him in a positive and supportive way, he could at least get them to communicate the negatives. If he could address those negatives, he could begin to earn their trust and change their attitudes.

Charlie then explained what parts of the new plan his team had accomplished. He described the architecture changes, the roles his team members were playing, and the structures they were putting in place to define lines of communication, escalation, and prioritization. "Where I really need each of you to work with me," Charlie said, "is in merging the ideal vision you have in your mind for how things should work with the best practices and use cases our vendors are bringing to the table." Several of the people in the room visibly bristled at this statement.

"Before you react to that, let me explain what I mean. No matter what, we need to ensure that the requirements we define and the priorities we set are aligned with what each of you needs at each step. I don't see this as a moon shot. If you folks don't see benefits to your operations in each iteration, then what's the point in this exercise? We all know the problems we need to solve for the sake of the business. Your input will drive how we go about solving them."

He had their attention at the least.

"The technology we're using has taken on these kinds of challenges before. In some cases Commapps – and Al Marcus in particular – will know how to best accomplish what you're trying to do, even if it doesn't look exactly like what you'd envisioned." More bristling, but the attendees were interested.

"In many cases, we'll get you exactly what you want or better. But there will be times where I'm going to tell you to throttle back what you're asking for, or to test out a different approach. Typically I will do this for timing and cost reasons. We do not want to over-customize these new platforms. We want to go with the flow. By doing this iteratively, and engaging in these workshops, you'll have a chance to nudge things where you want them. You certainly won't have something you can't live with forced on you."

As Charlie opened the discussion, several questions emerged from around the room. They were aggressive in some cases, and often dubious, but Charlie sensed the business managers were willing to talk. He knew he could turn that energy into something positive. Several people wanted to understand how the new architecture would make things simpler for them. They were concerned about disruptions to their processes; the amount of time their staff might be pulled away to work on requirements and testing; and the amount of training that would be required.

"I won't lie to you," Charlie said. "One of the real risks we're facing is a lack of subject matter expertise. A lot of people in the IT group who had knowledge we could use have left. That means we'll need to turn to you and your people for help. But understand that we're not looking to move today's processes onto the new platform as-is. We need to go through some amount of process re-engineering. We'll ask you to lend some of your best people to ongoing requirements workshops and ultimately to focus groups that will test the new systems before they go live. I think you'll see though, especially as we progress in these meetings, that those little sacrifices will deliver long term rewards."

A few foreheads wrinkled at this suggestion.

"But I don't expect you all to take my word for that just yet."

Some of wrinkles turned to smiles and nods. But several heads in the room began to shake and some quiet, frustrated groans could be heard.

"Hear me out for a minute," Charlie said with emphasis. "We need to do some re-engineering, but that's why I keep saying that your needs drive our requirements. You know what works and what needs improvement. You know where your costs are that you want to minimize. You know where your bottlenecks are. And you know that in many cases the systems you're using today, while basically functional, aren't up to par with our competitors. They don't even let you sell to or keep customers well enough to beat your quotas. I've heard most of you agree to that point."

No one could disagree. They didn't love the idea of major changes, but they did like the prospect of major improvements. They just weren't sure yet that IT could deliver them.

One of the directors from video marketing raised a hand and Charlie nodded to him. "I hear what you're saying Charlie. We all know we're losing in the marketplace and need to make changes to fix that. I think guys that if our people make the effort to guide Charlie's folks then the odds are pretty good they'll deliver for us. Brad didn't involve any of us, so let's at least recognize that cooperation seems to make sense. If we do this incrementally we won't ask too much for our teams or force too much change all at once."

"That's fair enough," a junior VP from the Internet product group offered, "but we're also talking about making this happen in a tight window. So I like the philosophy, I'm just struggling to see how we do this step by step if we have to rush. This sounds risky to me."

"Look," Charlie said, "I know none of you wants your name on something that might blow up in your face. But I also know you don't want to be out on the street looking for jobs with a failed company on your résumé. You're all still here because you've got a lot of time and energy invested in this company. Speed is a concern, but my core team has done exactly what I'm talking about in just as tight a time frame and delivered some of the best solutions in world. I know I need to prove to you that I'm not going to make the same mistakes as my predecessor. That's fine. All I'm asking of each of you right now is to communicate with me and my people and give us a chance to work and deliver for you."

The room was silent for a few moments as everyone soaked in what Charlie had just vigorously presented to them. He had a point. Everyone in that room had something to lose and had been frustrated when Forrester ran wild without communicating. They all wanted to see if Charlie would stand by his words, but what he'd said made sense. The company was suffering, and ultimately they were responsible for changing it. If they wanted to succeed, and compete in the marketplace, they'd need to improve the way they did business. IT could be a catalyst for this if it was pointed in the same direction as the business. With a year in the hole because of Forrester, there was a lot of ground to make up.

"Charlie," one of the senior managers from the voice services unit began to ask, "How are you going to make sure this thing stays focused on what we need? I've heard the open communications pitch before, but I've seen these kinds of projects get pork barreled to death, or turn into a bunch of disconnected skunk works," – heads began to nod in agreement. "How will you avoid that?"

"I'm actually glad you asked," Charlie replied. "First, understand that I don't fall in love with technology. It's a means to an end, and that end is business. My grand vision is measured in dollars, not in the number of lines of code my guys can write." A few people in the room smirked, those that understood the reference to Forrester.

"But don't take my word for it. We already have a process defined for dealing with scope changes. I've brought Al Marcus in from Commapps to work with Jim Taylor in the PMO. It's their job to scrutinize every request and to push back on anything that's extraneous. Al doesn't mind being a bad guy, and he's not afraid of a fight. The philosophy is simple – if it doesn't line up with the stated business goals, we just don't do it. Further, I'm engaging Lang Willis to assign a member of his team to be a liaison to our program. We'll have fiscal oversight on this. If something gets past Al and Jim that doesn't have a business case Lang's organization can approve, it won't be funded."

This caught everyone's attention. Charlie meant what he said about being open and enforcing transparency. They could see he was serious about doing things right, and lean, and in a business-driven manner. As Charlie looked around the room, he could see his audience was intrigued, listening, and reacting positively to him. There were a few stragglers, like some of the folks from wireless sales. They were in the back of the room, nodding here and there, but scowling or drifting more often. Charlie's work wasn't done, but he'd begun the process of engaging the business and getting them to pull in the same direction. Now he had to maintain that momentum, which meant delivering on what he'd promised them.

Monday, September 1st marked the official 90 day point for the program and thus the first Board review. Charlie had been chatting with Liz Fagan several times per day for the past week. She was increasingly anxious about what he would report. She had pressured him to focus on the revenue and market share projections she had summarized for the Board already. He tried to rein her in delicately. While he didn't think her projections were unrealistic, he knew there were risk factors and what-ifs to hedge against. In the end, his presentation was a compromise between their points of view. He was sure about his team's competence and progress. Fagan was encouraged because Charlie's team was a massive improvement compared to Forrester's. In the back of his mind though, promising aggressive revenue numbers this early in the game was ill advised.

The actual board meeting took place in the executive board room on the 42nd floor of the main building. The room's wrap around windows provided a stunning view of Unidigitel's campus which stood in an idyllic valley, surrounded by vineyards and farms. As Charlie spoke to the Board members, who were seated around a large, oval, polished wood table, he couldn't help but glance out of the window between slides at the inspiring sight.

Charlie had reviewed the disappointing findings from the discovery effort. He was careful to note that despite Liz Fagan's and Lang Willis' best efforts, Forrester had been deliberately deceptive about his lack of progress and budget burn rate. This financial debacle was now compounded by the $20 million write-down his team was recommending. Eliminating the third-party CRM component was costly, but it would also allow them to recover roughly $20 million in short term integration costs as well as tens of millions in long term maintenance costs and risk avoidance. The members of the Board weren't happy with the scenario, but saw the wisdom in Charlie's move to simplify the program and the immediate and long term benefits that would result.

Charlie explained how Michael Kim had joined his team from Lang Willis' office to oversee budget issues going forward. He described the executive steering committee he'd engaged to provide further oversight and critical decision making. He summarized the escalation procedures, status monitoring tools and policies that Miller and Jim had put in place, and the workshops he'd been conducting with business owners to revive the requirements gathering process and ensure alignment between the business units and IT.

He ran through the revised architecture plan, stressing the principles of operations simplification; elimination of any unnecessary custom development and integration work; and the expanded role of Commapps, which the Board members found to be prudent. He also shared the anecdote of how he'd levered Al Marcus onto his team and received laughs and muted applause for his cunning, puerile as it may have been. It was clear that Al's skill was paying off in the progress Charlie's team had made in setting the program back on track. Finally he turned to benefits realization.

"I want to thank you all for being patient in waiting for the punch line. The question you all want answered is, 'when will we see dollars result from all of this effort and investment.'" As he said this, he looked Roger Schultz, Chairman of the Board, directly in the eye. Schultz' gaze did not waver.

"I am confident that by April 1 next year we will have our primary contact centers running on our new web portal platforms with roll outs of our multi-service offerings delivered to three significant test markets. By June 1st, we will be in full production and will have begun our full data migration in earnest, which will in turn allow us to decommission a number of legacy systems. This chart shows the relationship between costs and benefits. You can see that July 1 represents the inflection point where benefits – i.e. revenue and profitability – should begin to overtake cost, which will decline dramatically with the majority of the development and deployment phases completed."

Benefits Realization

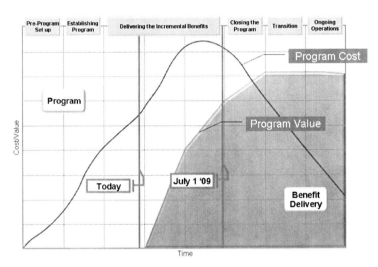

BENEFITS REALIZATION

As Charlie scanned the room he noticed a mix of intrigued and slightly confused looks. This was about what he'd expected.

"The thin line that looks like a roller coaster represents cost. As you can see, there was a significant increase in cost devoted to this program prior to my team's arrival. The area you see that's shaded in, where it says 'Benefit Delivery' represents the benefits we expect to derive from our restructured investments and activities. Early on we expect there will be little return for the amount of cost involved because of all of the changes that will be needed to realign and restructure the program. There is still too much complexity, too much wasted cost, and little governance. As we address these variables and right the ship, we expect, as I said, to see the benefits we can realize escalate rapidly. Ultimately, we should massively reduce the operational cost base and drive new revenue that will offset, recover, and surpass the overall cost of the program."

Charlie didn't lack confidence as he delivered his message, but he knew this was the point of no return. His future with Unidigitel, and possibly his legacy as a CIO, would be tied to whether he delivered on these promises. It was a tight schedule with high expectations. There were bound to be many hurdles along the way, regardless of how thorough his team was proving to be. Schultz and the other Board members weren't likely to be forgiving to him, or to Liz Fagan, after what Forrester had left them with. From here out, anything that went wrong would have nothing to do with Forrester in their minds. Charlie and Liz were on the hook for it all. One thing he knew for sure – June 1st, when he would present hard results to the Board, was going to be a very interesting day.

Dos and Don'ts for Chapter 4	
DO:	**DON'T:**
Prioritize business requirements against business goals and outcomes.	Forget to revisit regularly what the programs goals and objectives are, especially as they evolve over time.
Communicate program issues, problems and delays in a timely and comprehensive fashion.	Exclude stakeholders, even if they are resistant to the changes you're bringing.
Know the business and the reasons or business case behind the program effort.	
Have the elevator speeches ready on how the program is going.	
Thank the folks, especially those outside IT, for their help.	
Expose the benefits that justified the project and promote the business case.	

For more information on how EMC Consulting can assist you with your transformation visit: - **www.emc.com/services**

CHAPTER 5

Having spent years working as a consultant, Jim Taylor was accustomed to hitting the ground running on new projects. It was no surprise to Marc Miller that his friend was mostly up to speed within his first week on the job. Miller's administrative staff had already begun the trend of hanging climbing gear and arctic photos in his office. It was Jim Taylor, less than a week into his tenure, who had dressed a mannequin as a Sherpa and put it in Miller's doorway late one night. It was Jim's own way of telling his long time friend that he was glad to be on his team for the long haul this time.

Taylor's job was well defined. He was responsible for establishing a clear structure for the PMO. He would put tools and processes in place to make it easy for the project teams to report status, escalate problems and risk issues to himself and Miller, and to maintain visibility across other projects on which they were dependent. This structure was intended to empower people within the program to do their jobs, contribute ideas, anticipate problems, and offer solutions upstream and to peers in other areas. Visibility across projects would also help to create the critical sense of urgency needed to meet the aggressive deadlines everyone involved faced.

"What I'm seeing so far doesn't surprise me," Jim told Charlie and Miller in a summary email he scripted while flying back to Charlotte during the weekend of June 20th.

"Miller told me to expect most of this, but here's what I see thus far:
- Status goes from green to red: There's no warning system; No "yellow".
- Hardware procurement is a mess with 3 month turn around times.
- Project teams aren't empowered. All decision making went through the CIO.

- Issues logs are lengthy and aging. This is the result of overly centralized decision making. Teams hesitated to move on simple problems and there was no means of prioritizing, rating, or tracking status on open issues.
- Little urgency. Project deadlines slipped every week. Teams lost focus, momentum, and confidence due to constant changes coming from the PMO.
- Good news:
- Seen it and fixed it all before.
- Forrester left us good dashboard and report sharing apps; just didn't use them right.
- In initial discussions, several project managers seemed eager to get it right.

Taylor had a playbook he liked to follow for this sort of job and he planned to execute it. Miller was one of the managers who'd helped him develop it, so he had no objections. It was part of the reason Miller wanted him on board – the two could already anticipate each other's moves. Jim started by instituting a weekly "all hands on deck" call for the project managers. The first call was dedicated to defining the overall program structure for the group, giving them hard examples of how the reporting structure would work, how their individual projects interrelated, and what services and functions the PMO would provide.

The next three or four of these calls would be somewhat lengthy because they'd be devoted to prioritizing the aging issue logs and bringing them up to date. He also needed the managers to formulate a plan for using the collaboration and status dashboard tools Forrester had set up but not rolled out to his teams. This needed to happen no later than July 15th. This would then free them up to use the weekly calls to address issues that went beyond status reporting and risk identification. The calls could focus on issues that impacted key dependencies across the teams and could serve as mini-workshops where managers could help each other solve problems and find ways to reinvigorate staff members who'd been burned out or demoralized under Forrester.

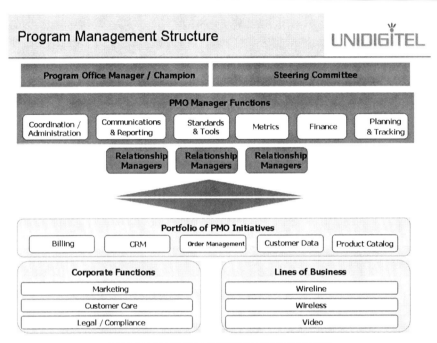

PROGRAM MANAGEMENT STRUCTURE

One of Taylor's mandates was that the project managers require their team members to use the documentation tools they'd bring online. Jim knew that turnover could kill a project. If a project relied on the knowledge stored in certain people's minds, it created untenable risks. The teams were not in the habit of documenting everything, so Taylor reinforced the need every day to the project managers. After a quick email exchange with Miller and Charlie, he was able to tell the managers they could earn points on their annual bonuses by following this golden rule.

Just before a break for the July 4th holiday, Charlie had promised Jim Taylor that he would recruit key individuals to participate in the executive steering committee. The committee would oversee the program's budget and activities. It would serve as the highest point of escalation for issues that would impact the program's scope, cost, or timeline. It was a critical piece of Taylor's playbook and he was pleased to see that the CIO was willing to make it a personal priority.

The program had been tainted under Forrester. Most of the executives knew that Dowd and his team wanted to move things in a more responsible and engaging direction, but that didn't mean they wanted to be the first to lend a hand. Some invitees, like CFO Lang Willis, pressed for this level of oversight. Others, like Rod Bender, head of sales, wanted to be in the know, but didn't want to be associated with anything that might fail. Charlie had to find hooks, and in some cases champions from the business, to help him pull in everyone he needed.

Brian Walker hadn't been with the company much longer than Charlie had. He was named Senior Vice President – Customer Care, Service, and Support in early March after the previous SVP left for a another company. He'd been promoted rapidly into the SVP position and was only 32. Charlie had received a text message from Walker during his first week with the company that read, "Stop by some time soon. 35th floor. Let's work 2gether."

He and Charlie had exchanged several emails, met for lunch a few times, and had developed a solid working relationship by the beginning of June. Walker was proving to be a useful source of information about customer support processes. He was committed, obsessed even, with the idea of migrating to one, do-all contact center that would be the "best in the world." Charlie appreciated the young executive's enthusiasm, but he wanted to temper it somewhat. He also knew that Walker wasn't entirely genuine. He was a nice enough person, but he had an agenda and it seemed to Charlie that his friendly outreach was born as much of manipulation as collegiality.

This was becoming more evident on Tuesday in the last week of July when Charlie hadn't received a response from Walker that he'd expected by the end of the previous week. He'd been distracted with helping the program team come together, so was only just following up. Walker liked to send texts, so Charlie followed suit. The two exchanged several messages within minutes.

> *Charlie: "R u on board?"*
> *Brian: "With what?"*
> *Charlie: "Asked u last Mon re exec comm."*
> *Brian: "Got questions. Can u stop by now?"*
> *Charlie: "5 mins."*

Charlie stepped into Walker's office without knocking exactly four minutes later. He didn't like playing these games.

"Charlie it's a pleasure," Walker said with an over eager smile. "How's it treating you today?"

"C'mon Brian, don't jerk me around. What's the issue?"

"Well, you said last week that you wanted me to join this executive steering committee, and I'm fine with that. My organization is going to be affected by the things yours is building and I want to have real input in that process," Walker said.

"And we're working with your people every day. What's the problem?"

"You said you also wanted me to help keep the sales and billing folks bought in. So are you asking me to join the committee, or champion your cause?" Walker pressed him.

"Well, a bit of both Brian. I thought we've gotten to know each other pretty well. I figured it would be worth your while to help sell my story since what you want and what I need to do are dependent on each other."

"That's true," Walker replied. "But how do I know you'll do what I need done once you get these other folks in the fold. I mean, I've spent a lot of time and effort to build trust with those guys. I have capital here. If you want to borrow it, that's fine. But what guarantees do I get in return?"

Charlie would have respected Walker more for being frank if he wasn't being a bit arrogant in the process. He chalked it up to youth and said, "Look, it goes without saying that there's quid pro quo here. You want your call center. Our web portal effort is central to that. It's already a priority. You'll be on this committee. You'll have access to any workshop you want. You can talk to me. If you're worried your stuff won't be prioritized, well don't. Take my word for it. And if not, then participate. If you see something you don't like, come straight to me with it. I'll bring it to Miller's attention. Now what else can I tell you about the committee?"

"How will it work and what'll its responsibilities be?"

"As I think I said before, it'll be the ultimate point of escalation for any major change items, budget issues, or organizational conflicts. The committee will have the final say on these major decisions. I'll also expect the members to remain informed about the status, at the least, of those aspects of the program that impact their organizations. If possible, the committee members should aim to head off any issues they find before they even manage to escalate. If that's not possible, then I'll ask you to communicate with me so we introduce these issues to the other committee members prior to our meetings and have options already fleshed out for everyone to consider and then decide or vote on."

"Okay. Who else is involved?"

"Our CFO, Lang Willis; the head of network; the new chief of billing; and myself as chairperson. After that it's you, and ideally the head of sales and the head of the audit committee though I haven't gotten the official word from either of them yet."

"When's the first meeting?"

"You'll get a meeting note sometime today about a call and then I'm going to try to get the whole group together face to face in the next couple of weeks, assuming we can get everyone in the same place at the same time. After that, we'll hold meetings every two weeks, unless an issue comes up that needs immediate attention."

"Alright. If you want me to talk to Bender, the head of sales…"

"I know him Brian," Charlie interjected.

"Well, I'll talk to him for you and warm him up so you can wrangle him."

"That's all I'm asking. Thank you."

As Charlie's 90-day Board review approached in late August, there was significant angst around options for the CRM platform. Earl and Al agreed that from the architectural point of view, using Commapps' pre-integrated CRM solution made obvious sense. It would eliminate problematic custom coding, integration work, and performance difficulties related to moving orders out of Forrester's choice of CRM platform and into the billing solution.

From a risk point of view, it would mean one less vendor to manage and would eliminate internal competition between two major rivals – the CRM provider and Commapps. It would also minimize long term risks and costs involved in maintaining the custom integration between the platforms. Not having to customize and redesign the CRM implementation would save the program three month's work or more while cutting head-count by nearly a dozen contractors and consultants. No stakeholders would be impacted because nothing had yet been rolled out.

The CFO's office had a different point of view. The CRM platform was where Forrester had blown his budget wide open, but obfuscated invoices and payments. There was little result functionally because his requirements changed continuously. The CRM vendor had fed off the chaos and billed for every change of direction. Michael Kim, rightly watching his organization's back, argued that a $20 million write down would be an embarrassment to the CFO and CEO.

"Charlie can dodge this bullet because it didn't happen on his watch," Kim argued to Jim Taylor in a frustrated email rant. "But it'll hit Lang, and Liz, right between the eyes. Earl and I discussed this. He's willing to put the numbers together to show how much we save in the long run by making this move.

But between what we've paid the CRM vendor, what we still owe, and the buy-out clause in their contract, it's a massive cash layout up front. Lang and I aren't willing to just sign off on it. You need to present us with another option or Lang's going to bring this to a head at the Board review."

Taylor didn't like being threatened, but he recognized that Kim was in a horrible position. Fiscal oversight of the program was his job and this was the biggest egg he was going to be asked to swallow. If he had just taken it, he'd be undermining his own role. Taylor wrote back:

"Mike - The other technical option is to keep the CRM piece in place and take on all the cost and risk of making it work. We can't bite that bullet for political reasons. But the right business move is to escalate this to the steering committee. Lang's on it. He can say his piece and the committee can do what's it's meant to do. Fair enough?"

"I'll let Lang know what to expect," was all Michael Kim wrote in reply.

Jim didn't wait for the next 7 a.m. meeting to call Charlie Dowd on this one. He'd forwarded Mike's emails to Miller who told him to, "Call Charlie now." Charlie's response was simple. He thanked Jim for bringing it to his attention immediately. He asked Jim to review Earl's long term cost analysis and deliver it to him within 24 hours with a summary of what the two technical options would be. He also asked Jim to get him Mike's notes in regards to payments made to the CRM vendor, outstanding invoices, and the buy-out clause in its contract. He then brought all of this information to Lang Willis' attention and let him know it was the prime item on the slate for an impromptu steering committee call he was pulling together before the end of the week. This decision had to be made and settled prior to the Board review.

"You realize Charlie that I'm going to object to this," Willis said.

"I do," Charlie answered.

"I can't just sign off on a $20 million write down."

"Of course not."

"If the rest of the committee agrees with you, and they probably will because they know Forrester messed this up, I'll abstain from voting on it rather than voting against it. But I have to take the position that IT dug this hole, and IT needs to deal with it. I don't care who was in charge at the time."

"I understand…"

Willis held up a hand. "Don't thank me Charlie. You may have to eat this one yet."

The steering committee convened via conference bridge on Thursday, August 28th. Charlie made his case for replacing the CRM component outright. He played to the needs of sales, care, and marketing. He told them call center consolidation and the new web-based sales, care and support tools wouldn't be deliverable without this move. He convinced the marketing and sales chiefs that they'd be able to roll their new offerings three months sooner as a result of the change. He pitched Lang, already knowing his position, on the long term cost savings and risk reduction benefits. The executive vice president of network operations, Barry Word, wasn't an affected stakeholder in any way. He appreciated the position Charlie was in and didn't intend to oppose him. Liz Fagan wasn't on the call due to a prior commitment, but had replied to the Outlook request for the meeting with a note that gave Charlie her full confidence.

"For the record," Lang Willis chimed in when Charlie had finished making his pitch, "I think that if IT made this bed, IT should sleep in it."

"Lang, this was Brad's doing…" Lila Green, head of the audit committee interjected.

"I understand that. But to me it's all the same IT pot. I can't see the logic in throwing away a $20 million asset. I don't buy all of the integration mumbo-jumbo and I see Commapps pulling the strings in the background. I'm sorry Dowd, that's just how I see it. I recognize this committee needs to vote on the final decision. That's why we're here. I know most of you will benefit from Charlie's strategy and could care less about his budget issues. I don't have that luxury. I'll accept whatever decision you all choose to make, but up front I want to say that I am opposed to this. Forrester lied to my organization. What IT is asking for now is a bail out. I won't sign off on it. The members of this committee will have to accept responsibility for it."

There was a prolonged silence as the participants on the call mulled over Willis' comments. After nearly a minute, Brian Walker spoke first.

"Time to vote folks. I can't see any option but to take the write down. The pros outweigh the cons, even if the many cons are tough to swallow." Walker shot Charlie a look that said, "You owe me one…a big one."

Each member of the committee said his or her piece briefly. In the end the decision was made to follow Charlie's recommendation, but not without some hesitation after Willis' words. Charlie had gotten the answer he needed, but wasn't sure he'd necessarily won a battle in the process. His head was on the chopping block most of all if this decision proved to be the wrong one.

September 17th was Pat Morton's birthday, but no one knew it. She didn't like a fuss. This year, her birthday was proving to be a lousy one. She'd received a series of text pages at 4 a.m. alerting her that Unidigitel's primary server vendor had suffered a fire at its primary distribution hub that would impact all requests for new hardware. Marc Miller was online by 6 a.m. from home and immediately saw an email from Pat Morton and a status alert in his inbox.

The CRM working group's status had gone yellow to signify a jeopardy situation. Pat Morton's email asked for an immediate call regarding a hardware supply problem she needed to explain in person. He text paged her immediately saying, "I'll be in my office by 7. Please meet me there." He then text messaged Jim and Earl and told them he expected them there too. As usual on Wednesdays, they'd been there since 5:30 a.m. dealing with issue logs and requirements requests, drinking coffee and eating egg sandwiches.

Pat hustled into Miller's office at five minutes past seven and came face to face with the Sherpa guarding the door. "You gotta get rid of that thing. It's hideous," she said to everyone in the room.

"Hey, that Sherpa is the most reliable employee I've ever had," Miller retorted without looking up from the dashboard he was examining. Looking up over the edge of his glasses he said, "Tell me what's up."

"We have a problem."

"Tell the Sherpa, he's the complaint department," Campbell quipped from behind a newspaper.

"Shut up Earl, I said a problem, not a complaint."

"In that case, it's Taylor's job."

"What's my job?" Jim Taylor said, returning to the office with four bottles of water."

"Apparently it's waterboy," Morton said without missing a beat. Taylor smirked in response.

"I lost a bet… What's happening?"

"We have a hardware problem. I got a text page late last night from the vendor and the CRM working group leader must have also because I got an alert from them too."

"Yeah, I was going to check in with those folks in a just a bit. They've gone 'yellow' and I wanted to see what their hold up is. We need those new CRM components to be accelerating to catch up, not falling further behind."

"Right," Morton picked up the conversation, "that yellow ought to be a red. The problem isn't with the software. It's a supply issue. I called our rep with the server vendor on my way over here. We can lean on them all we want, they don't have the gear we need and won't for months. They have a lot of demand for the product so there's no surplus lying around. Their distribution center in Chennai was caught in a fire from an adjacent warehouse last night, or yesterday. It's a mess."

"I don't suppose we predicted that in the risk plan specifically, but Earl I'm assuming you've accounted for supply issues. What's the contingency plan?"

"I'd say we go to another vendor," Earl answered.

"No, but that's the issue," Morton said. "We can use Saturn Micro's boxes. From an application point of view, it won't make a difference. We can get that hardware right away, but the company isn't a preferred supplier and we're looking at about a 15 percent cost premium there. We'll also have the data center guys pushing back at us. They've been fighting the good fight all along to keep their environment pretty standard, so it'll take some wrangling to get those guys to play ball. That's outside of our direct authority. We can't just dictate to them."

"They report to network. Head of network is on the steering committee. Do we need Charlie to get involved on that level?" Jim asked.

"I can brief him and let him decide," Miller said. "What are our other options?"

"As I see it, there aren't any. We either wait about three months and delay CRM a whole quarter but keep the data center happy. Or, we get the data center guys bent out of shape about introducing and supporting hardware they're not familiar with, spend some more money, but keep the program on schedule."

"Well that's a no brainer, but it's not actually our call," Miller said. "This goes up to the committee. We're talking timeframe, deliverables, budget, supply chain issues, other organizations being impacted. This is their turf. Let Charlie know what's happening and let's make sure he's got all of the documentation he needs."

Later that day, Charlie Dowd set up a three-way call for himself, Brian Walker, and Barry Word, the EVP of network operations. He wanted to set the stage for the next steering committee meeting that was scheduled for the following week.

"Charlie, I saw the alert come up on my dashboard that the CRM piece is already in jeopardy," Walker said hurriedly. "My folks told me they can't get servers because someone burnt down a warehouse? Is that right?"

"That's what I understand and why I called you both."

"Brian, how are you?" Word asked in a husky baritone.

"Barry…"

"Gentlemen," Charlie interjected, "let me get right to the point. We can't get servers from our approved vendor for three months, but we can't delay our CRM project for three months either…"

"Then you better find that gear some other way," Word said defensively. "I won't agree to you bringing foreign gear into the data centers. Those guys are finally making progress on a unified environment. It's been a nightmare for the past five years. I'm not willing to go back in the opposite direction on them."

"Barry, I'm not sure we have a choice here," Charlie said bluntly. "We can do this temporarily if that's what it comes to, but we can't delay the CRM side of this project for a full quarter and have any chance of it surviving. We can't tackle the call center unification without it. We can't make our production deadlines. And that means we can't start selling and showing revenue on the new platform. Liz and the Board would never stand for that over a basic hardware issue. We'll owe you. I get that. But we need you to take one for the team right now."

"If there are added costs in procuring and maintaining that gear, I'm willing to share some budget from my side. Don't worry about that," Walker offered. "We've been running leaner for a few months now. I have a little breathing room."

"I'm in decent shape if you owe me a favor Charlie," Word admitted. "Let's say I'll just make sure I cash it in before they dismiss you." Charlie wasn't sure if he was kidding or not. "And Brian, I'll take you up on that offer. My folks will kick and scream, so you guys will have to pay for the bonus I'll want to pay them for playing nice with the CRM guys. But that's not the favor you owe me. That's the table stakes."

"Fair enough," Charlie replied. Then he began to sweat. Two weeks ago he'd made promises to the Board and had a sinking feeling something was going to go wrong. He was thinking now that he should have trusted his instincts and reined in his, and Liz Fagan's, optimism.

The following week, with most of the members of the executive steering committee gathered in the board room on the 42nd floor, Charlie Dowd laid out two options for dealing with the hardware supply problem that cropped up. He had delivered a well vetted case to the other members of the committee prior to the meeting, so everyone already knew that the vote was either for "wait" or "go" and knew how dependent projects and the budget would be affected by either decision. Waiting meant keeping the budget in check and not taking a step backwards in the improving data centers. But it would delay one of the program's primary thrusts in delivering a common, web-based sales and care platform.

"You know, what I don't like about this scenario is that we have procurement processes in place for a reason. When we step outside them we expose ourselves to risks and distractions we don't need," said Lila Green, the chairperson of the audit committee.

"My concern is that we're not putting something in that's aligned with our long term plan. It'll mean the boxes that run my new sales applications are going to be red headed step children in the data center," added Rod Bender, head of sales.

"I had the same concern," Walker replied, "but that's why Barry's idea about an incentive makes sense to me."

"Incidentally," Charlie inserted, "Mike Kim confirmed for me that IT can fund it out of our reserve."

"I need these new applications up on time to make my contact center consolidation happen, so I don't see why we need to give in to a religious war in the data center," Walker added. He might have said too much.

"Look Brian, you weren't here while we spent five years fighting every battle to consolidate the data centers and normalize them down to just a few common platforms. That was a Herculean effort and my guys deserve the kudos they've gotten for it. I support the fact that the business needs these deadlines to be made, and I recognize that means my team will be impacted. Hence the bonus incentive. But let's at least agree it's a step in the wrong direction for us as much as a necessary step forward for Charlie's group."

Langdon Willis III, CFO, cleared his throat and silenced the buzzing room. "I would be reluctant to add funds to this effort, though Mike Kim also assured me IT has the reserve to cover it – in the short term anyway. I'm ticked that CRM is cropping up again as a problem after that write down. But Charlie's teams are on target right now. I can't see the sense in delaying half the project because the folks we pay in the data center don't like the label on the computers you want to buy. I'll approve it. The bonus idea makes sense though I want to look closely at the numbers and the triggers tied to it. I'll sign off on this. But Dowd, you know you're on thin ice."

With less than two weeks until Christmas, Jim Taylor was sitting in the spot he'd carved out for himself in Miller's office. He was taking a few minutes to shop online for gifts for his folks and his sister's family when he received an alert on his management dashboard that told him the data migration project was in jeopardy. It was followed shortly thereafter by an email from Earl Campbell that read:

"Jimmy-
Check your dashboard. We have a bigger data problem than you thought.
-Campbell"

Taylor took a minute to finish entering his credit card number into a web site to ship a box full of toys to his niece and nephew before replying to Campbell:

"What did you do now?
I'm in Miller's office – stop by.
- Taylor"

Campbell's news was pretty bad. The whole team knew that data migration was almost always one of the most problematic aspects of any major IT conversion. But Campbell had found that even the most pessimistic estimates had been incorrect. There was no way around an extensive manual scrub of the data that needed to move into the customer data hub and feed both the CRM and billing processes.

This was a long term issue that would largely affect the program's year two plans, but it also threatened production deadlines. Certain subsets of customers needed to be identified and moved into the new system to support initial market launches. Also, the stage needed to be set for federating existing data stores and migrating in an organic way those customers who took up new offerings. Both of those goals were undermined based on Campbell's finding that even with automated data cleansing tools and validation against clean, 3rd party data, customer identification and matching had a greater than 30 percent error rate. Using a largely manual process, someone would have to scrub tens of millions of records across multiple databases. This would inevitably delay the launch and add significant cost to the budget.

Taylor reached Marc Miller with a text message that read:

- I need you and Charlie on a data problem. 911. -

Within an hour, Charlie, Miller, Earl Campbell and Jim sat around a table in Charlie's office to figure their options.

"The good news Charlie is that we already have a plan for how to deal with this without completely exploding the budget, but it will mean shifting some responsibilities around," Taylor told him.

"What does it do the schedule? Tell me that first," Charlie insisted. First the CRM issue had cropped up, and now this problem. His instinct had been correct at the Board review. He'd promised a bit too much.

"It likely pushes everything back one month," Taylor told him.

"Is that a conservative estimate?"

"Let's say a pessimistic estimate would be six weeks, if we go with the alternate plan," Miller offered.

"Okay, tell me the plan," Charlie said.

"Well, MasterDat has an offshore shop that specializes in this kind of work," Taylor told him. "What we could do is have them not only handle the scrubbing, but give them the migration work too. That means we pull some work away from ITSI and Commapps, but we get all of that work done for the same price. I need to make some calls to confirm that, but I had a quick chat with the account rep before I ran over here and he was comfortable with it. He was happy to win some more business to say the least."

"Alright," Charlie said, rubbing both hands over his head and thinking out the variables. First, I'll need to talk to Al about this because it impacts him. ITSI wouldn't really be hit by this until next summer. Marc, you can take care of them. I need a real answer on what this does to the budget though. The idea basically makes sense to me, but I'll have to go to the committee on this. We can't send our core customer data offshore without buy-in from them. A month or so delay isn't the end of the world, but it's a black mark for us. I'll have to take some heat for this."

"Chief, this is on me," Miller said. "My initial estimate was off. Put it on my head if you have to."

"No, this is on me Marc. I knew at the Board review that I wasn't accounting for a delay like this. I was trying to back up the dates and numbers Liz was pushing. Now I'll pay for not listening to myself. Let's just make sure we do everything we can to minimize this. It basically leaves us with no margin for error from here out."

Two days later, with Al Marcus visibly irritated for once, confirmation that the offshore option was feasible, and a security plan for protecting the sensitive data involved in the project, Charlie contacted the steering committee members to prep them for the next meeting. Their reactions were mixed. Lila Green hated the idea of sending customer data out of house, regardless of how strong the security plan and contracts might be. Lang Willis was pleased he wasn't being asked for more budget. Brian Walker was disappointed about the delay, but agreed the solution Charlie had offered made sense. Barry Word understood that solving this problem now eliminated a long term risk factor for the company and supported the effort.

Rod Bender, ever the squeaky wheel, agreed with Green's position. "I don't want some mole over there stealing my customer info and selling it to a competitor," he blustered.

"These guys do this kind of work all the time Rod. They are certified in every way possible. There's no more risk in their shop than there would be in ours, especially given the number of contractors that have been coming and going for the past year and half," Charlie argued.

Ultimately, Liz Fagan held the decisive vote. She was in Paris speaking at an executive leadership conference and responded to Charlie via email:

Charlie-
First, I probably should apologize for pressuring you over the launch dates and numbers. I think you tried to tell me and I didn't listen very well. We're in this pickle together. I think

your team's fix is sound. I'm impressed at how well they responded. You've built a heck of a team and that will make all the difference in the end. I'll talk to Roger and some of the other Board members about this so it doesn't come as a surprise. In the meantime – press on. I support your plan, so let's not waste another day deliberating over it. This is my call. Press go.

Regards,

Liz

Dos and Don'ts for Chapter 5	
DO:	**DON'T:**
Put in place processes to capture program knowledge.	Put a steering committee in place without articulating its explicit purpose and goals, how it operates, and the mechanisms it will use.
Constantly transfer the tacit knowledge in individuals' heads into explicit documentation	Grind so hard that you alienate or burn out your people.
Pace your teams. Grind when necessary, but otherwise set a reasonable tempo.	

For more information on how EMC Consulting can assist you with your transformation visit: - **www.emc.com/services**

CHAPTER 6

Earl Campbell often sat alone in the cafeteria's corner. He didn't welcome company. Very few people liked the curmudgeon. He was too much the straight shooter. Too often he ripped others for their shortcomings when his own could fill a warehouse. He could be funny and engaging with his peers, but subordinates rarely knew when he was kidding and when his biting repartee was serious. So, when Gail Sawyer, who Earl had had known and respected for nearly 10 years, sat down across the table, he didn't assume it meant trouble, but he was suspicious.

"I'd like to chat with you for a minute Earl," she said.

"Is there a problem with your project you need to air out?" he asked with feigned patience.

"You could say that. I just talked to Marc Miller to let him know I'm leaving."

"You're bailing out on us?" Campbell sneered derisively.

"No Earl, it's not like that at all. My daughter is having a baby. She wants me to be there to help her, so I've decided to retire. I'm moving to Santa Fe."

"I see. Well, I guess I'll have to admit to being a bit envious. And I guess I should say…congratulations? Or, happy grandparent's day? Is that what you say?"

"Something like that. Thank you."

"Okay, well, what can we do about replacing you?" He cut right to the point.

"Your sensitivity knows no bounds…I did what Jim had asked of all the project mangers in the beginning and I've documented everything and organized it in the knowledge base the way it's supposed to be."

Early on, Jim, Earl and Miller knew that attrition was one of the biggest risks their program would face. Many of the more talented folks who'd toiled under Forrester's misdirected leadership had left for other opportunities or were on the verge of jumping ship.

Jim Taylor had driven home the point again and again that he didn't want to rely on what he called "heroics." The program couldn't depend too heavily on any one individual. Information about specific projects couldn't hide in someone's head or on their laptop. Documentation processes and shared knowledge repositories were necessary to capture as much information about the individual projects as possible. These could help to ensure continuity as project managers and subject matter experts, like Gail Sawyer, entered and exited the program.

Being a veteran and a team player, Sawyer was thorough. She provided background on her project and team; recording her team's activities; budget impact; timelines; supplier and support contacts; and status and details behind outstanding work items. She even went so far as to leave suggestions to whoever would take her place as to the best way to motivate certain individuals. Her team was sorry to see her go, but her reasons made the parting simpler than cases where a key player left for a competitor, which had happened too often in Forrester's wake.

Gail pushed her tray aside and placed her laptop on the table to begin an impromptu presentation of what she was leaving behind. She showed Earl where in the knowledge base all of her files were stored. In those files were all of the relevant artifacts relating to the analytics implementation she'd been managing. She had slides showing what each member of her team was responsible for; who reported to them and to whom they reported; summaries and detailed versions of her revised project plans; and an explanation of the project's issue escalation process and how it connected to the PMO.

Sawyer raised an outstanding issue that grabbed Campbell's attention. The first was that the debate over what to do about the hardware shortage had delayed her moving her application from a low volume development environment into a high volume test environment. This application should have been relatively straightforward to install alongside the billing system. Its complexity was in configuring it to analyze specific data and search for complex patterns in customer behavior.

The hardware issue wasn't something Sawyer had anticipated. Campbell was already aware of the issue though. He'd performed the analysis with Pat Morton on the hardware problem's impact on the schedule.

Sawyer's team was also facing a time sensitive personnel issue. Analytics was a new concept for everyone, so the team she'd been given had billing, customer care, and marketing experience, but none of them had worked with an analytics engine before. Commapps leant a subject matter expert who was helpful in providing technical knowledge of the product, but there wasn't anyone on the team who had the experience needed to be considered an obvious replacement for Sawyer.

When Campbell returned to Miller's office after lunch and his chat with Gail, he began thumbing through the risk plan to see what the contingency was for this kind of situation. To his surprise he found a succinct answer to his question: "ITSI Consulting." Bringing in an expert from ITSI would allow the analytics team to learn from an experienced expert who could both run the project and educate the team on intricacies of using an analytics solution. Campbell reminded himself to ask Gail which of her team members could become a good team leader once the implementation was finished and the application was put to work.

Earl's title was Chief Architect, but in the PMO's division of labor, he was also responsible for putting strong risk management controls, processes and tools in place. One of the reasons Forrester had banished Campbell was an email he'd written to the formed CIO. Campbell told him his program would fail because his risk plan was a joke and had no realistic contingencies; that it failed to establish any kind of continuous risk assessment; that his vendors weren't sharing any risk; and that despite taking on a huge technology project, Forrester had no plans for risk prototyping whatsoever.

Campbell knew when he began working for Miller that he'd have to examine a variety of interrelated risks. Risks in development; data integrity; performance; and conversion to the new solutions were obvious for any IT project and would be multiplicative in a program of this scope. Jim Taylor had offered Earl a high level risk management map to use as a basis for defining and documenting his risk management process. Campbell appreciated the gesture, though he teased Taylor about "his precious," referring to the playbook Taylor often kept close at hand.

Issue/Risk Management UNIDIGITEL

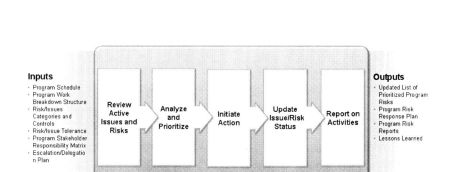

ISSUE/RISK MANAGEMENT

One of the risks he, Jim and Miller had attacked early on in redesigning the architecture was vendor delivery risk. Fewer vendors were now involved in the program and certain deals had been restructured to provide incentives and penalties relating to solution delivery. The risk Campbell was happy to have dealt with in detail the minute he said goodbye to Gail in the cafeteria related to an increasing lack of qualified SMEs to run and execute projects.

One of Campbell's strengths was identifying dependencies. As an experienced architect, he understood how to look at IT programs systemically and see how different technical and personnel issues could affect the whole. For any point in the program he always wanted to be able to answer the question, "If you press stop here, what happens to everything else?" This type of analysis drove his approach to risk assessment. He mapped out all of the program's dependencies and understood what was and was not within the program's control.

The latter were real risks, like talented people leaving or key suppliers failing to deliver for whatever reason. With these identified, Campbell had called a late night whiteboard session with Jim and Miller to do contingency planning and round out the first version of the risk plan. Hiring a replacement for Gail would be just one of the issues Campbell would have to rely on good planning and quick thinking to resolve in the coming months.

It was 7:12 a.m. on a Monday in late October. As he always was at this time, Earl was on the conference bridge with the rest of the program team waiting for his turn to report. Earl was just getting his head back into business after taking the weekend off. He'd worked the previous week with Al Marcus and one of Al's SMEs to kick the tires on a new digital rights management component that was going to be introduced to the architecture. Forrester had been evaluating several third party products, but hadn't ever made a final choice. Earl had cancelled several undocumented but ongoing proof of concept trials in the previous months. Right away, the SME had proven himself useful. From a risk perspective, Earl knew that going with Commapps' pre-integrated, though relatively new, DRM component would help simplify and thus de-risk the integration process. He also saw, however, that the solution would only get Unidigitel about 75 percent of what it needed. The SME had been up front about the solution's maturation process and some potential performance risks.

The performance risk related primarily to scale. The

first version of the DRM component was installed in several European and Asian accounts and was supporting both video and mobile content in several of them, but in separate, parallel installations. No one instance of the component was running more than about one million subscribers' worth of transaction volume. Unidigitel had more than 20 million subscribers. The DRM component would see three or four times the transaction volume it had in any other installation. The SME was "pretty sure" that scale would not be a problem with the right hardware approach. This put greater pressure on the hardware issue the program faced, but it wasn't a new problem.

The SME assured Earl that the DRM component had managed in lab tests five times more volume than it had seen anywhere in the field. Campbell knew though that production environments would often prove more demanding and idio-syncratic than the controlled conditions in the lab. The DRM component would play a role in ensuring that any video or audio content was protected properly before being down-loaded to a subscriber. Real time demands could cause transaction volumes to multiply exponentially. So Campbell had to have well defined contingencies to deal with a possi-ble, though unlikely, no-go scenario.

The greater issue the SME identified related to function-ality and could exacerbate the scale question. The require-ments called for the DRM system to recognize users across a variety of access methods. For example, a user might want to send a video from his DVR over to his mobile device. The DRM system would have to recognize this as a legitimate transaction and let it go, where other such viral content shar-ing would not be permitted without payment.

The SME admitted to Earl that this functionality would require some modifications to the solution's code. It would be nearly impossible to develop, test and prove it before the pro-gram's target launch date. The problem was, delaying it was complicated. The business owners were excited about being the first to bring this sharing feature to market. It had to be delivered to keep them bought in. A contingency that called for going live without this feature wasn't likely to fly.

"Earl, you had something to add on the risk front?" Charlie Dowd asked after receiving status updates from Miller, Jim, and Al Marcus.

"Right, well, Al conveniently forgot to mention…"

"I didn't forget mate, I just like to set you up…" Marcus quipped.

"Funny…as I was saying, Al failed to mention some issues we have with this new digital rights management component we're bringing in."

"DRM? I thought that was settled a couple of weeks ago," Charlie said.

"Well, we chose Al's solution. That's not the issue. I've been working with Al's expert on this thing. We have scale and functionality risks to deal with."

Campbell walked the team through the risk issues and explained in sufficient detail what he'd seen.

"Neither of those problems sounds unrecoverable. What's the mitigation plan for this?" Charlie asked Earl.

"I think we can tackle the scale issue head on," Campbell replied. "We need to test the application on our hardware. I've looked over Commapps' tests and I'm satisfied with what I've seen thus far, but I want to know that it'll run the same on our hardware. I also want to know that if we run into a volume issue, we can solve it with hardware and that it's not a fundamental problem where the software just won't scale."

"I'd think the hardware folks will help us there, no? They need to save face after what that fire did to us. I think they'll do whatever it takes, right?" Miller asked.

"Pat, you spoke with them on this. What'd they say?" Earl asked Pat Morton.

"They can put us in their test lab for now and have gear for us by the time we need to launch. We'll need to define the use cases a bit better, and we'll need the test harness from Commapps…"

"I'll get on that," Marcus commented.

"…but the hardware folks are on board." Pat Morton concluded.

"Okay. Then what's our plan for dealing with the new code?" Charlie persisted.

"I think we have a few options to consider," Earl replied. "The first is to tell the business owners that they just can't have this functionality. I don't think that's going to go over too well obviously."

There was assent mumbled across the call.

"Another option is to launch content sharing without the smarts. In other words, we'd launch parallel instances of the component for each service. When customers want to pull content from one device to another, they'll have to authenticate each transaction. That would minimize new code we'd have to write because it would cut out all the calls and checks you need to auto-authenticate the transactions. It's a little less elegant and calls for more button pushes, but it'll deliver the service. We can work on the 'smart' part and launch it when Commapps' new code is stable."

"I don't love the quick and dirty approach," Charlie responded.

"My concern here," Miller added, "is whether the business guys will still be in love with this thing six months from now. Instead of derailing what we're trying to do, I want to make sure they have a plan for bringing this functionality to market before we pay Commapps to build it."

"I agree," Charlie said. "If we're going to build it, they better need it and have a plan for it. But if they do, then we need to deliver. If we say we can launch the vanilla version first, and then give them the smart version six months down the road, it gives us options, but I'm not sure they'll accept that."

"Well, we could fast track the code and just launch it in a limited geography," Earl suggested. "Or we just do an alpha test on it at least before we go into full production. It's risky to do it this way though. We'd be more likely to fail entirely or roll something out that just isn't production ready."

"Let me ask you this Earl," Pat Morton cut in. "What happens if Commapps delivers the code but it doesn't pass our scale test? What then?"

"Well, we'd be in trouble…Okay, the contingency is that we've got data from the POCs we cancelled on some 3rd party products that can already do what we're asking. But I'd hate to see us go back to bolting on components. That adds a different sort of risk to the equation. I know the steering committee doesn't want to hear about spending more on this DRM piece or on integration. So our options are limited."

"I think the path sets itself then," Charlie stated. "We need to keep things on schedule, and I'm not chasing new code down a rabbit hole. So, we need to launch this thing like you said Earl, with some extra button pushes. The marketing and sales guys can still sell the content sharing service that way; it just won't be 100 percent like they envisioned it out of the gate. Parma and I will have to deal with them. Parma?"

"Yes sir." Parma replied.

"You think you're ready to take another crack at the wireless group?"

"I have a funny story I can share with you later about that, but yes. I think I can work with them a bit better now," she said.

"Good…"

"Question, if I may…" Al Marcus interjected. "Who's doing the development, and who's paying for it?"

"I'm glad you asked Al…" Charlie said.

"That doesn't sound good."

"Al, you're going to show us whose team you're really on. Here's the deal. I've dealt with this kind of issue many times before. I already know I'm going to want a, say, 6 month exclusivity deal if Commapps is going to develop this on our backs."

"I think I can get our company to develop it well enough. That's how we operate – we build things with customers and sell them to other customers. That's the business. The exclusivity deal…that'll be tricky."

"It's a must-have. The business owners will flip if they know we're building this so you guys can go sell it to our competitors. I won't let that happen. I want your guys to develop it AI, and I'm happy to let them sell it down the road, but I want six months exclusive."

"It might be limited to certain geographies. Like, we can sell the functionality to companies that don't compete with you, outside of the U.S. for example."

"I'd want a royalty deal on those sales," Charlie fired back. "We don't need a huge piece, and we don't want to get into a debate over what IP belongs to whoever, but we definitely want a heads up on who they're selling this to."

Al Marcus choked down an irritated retort, but assented. "You're not making my job any easier. I'm going to eat a lot of…"

"Save it Al. We've got an awful lot of money invested with you guys and you'll build and test this thing on our backs. Plus, I'll do the reference calls. I'll do the speaking engagements. No worries. I'm willing to give here. But you know my priority is to protect Unidigitel's interests get this done without busting the budget. If I'm going to be the lab rat, I need something to show for it."

By mid-December, as everyone but the core program team was planning what to do with their holiday time; Earl Campbell was wrestling with data migration risks. Unidigitel, like most of its peers, had evolved on a product-centric basis over time. Customer and product information, as well as processes were spread across many different organizations and systems. To achieve customer-centricity and have services span different network domains customer data needed to move to one location or become centrally accessible.

Miller's earliest data quality assessments suggested that data was relatively consistent within each silo. The systems in each area used different information and data models though. These would have to be normalized prior to migration. Miller had assumed the information could be transformed into a common format and that disparate information about the same customers could be matched and loaded in a relatively straightforward, if effort intensive, manner. Campbell suspected Miller's assumptions were off target.

Earl knew that the data in various legacy systems had been used and abused for many years. Data errors grew due to poor data entry and inconsistent updates. Information was outdated because, for example, customer addresses were not updated proactively and existing customers were lazily added as new customers under a different address.

Unidigitel had also changed its credit scoring process several years earlier. That change resulted in combinations of the old, simple coding system that rated customers as E for excellent, G for good, or P for poor, and the new system which included a customer's actual credit score. This information was mixed up and out of date.

Campbell also expected to find customer lifetime value and semantic alignment problems. The new billing and CRM systems took the customer lifetime value concept into account. They assigned a code to each customer based on their long term value to the company in terms of profitability. Gail Sawyer's analytics project was supposed crunch the data that would be used to generate these codes, but Earl already faced some delays with that project.

Semantic issues were tricky because scanning tools wouldn't always uncover them. For example, a customer's account could be tagged as "late in paying" after 30 days in one system, but after 60 days in another. To a scanning tool, either system could have a legitimate value in the account status field. But, values would be different for the same customer when it came time to match customer records for migration. Matching would be challenging because of the discrepancies in customer names and addresses across systems.

Earl insisted on data scanning and testing tools early on so that he could measure the data risks. Unidigitel had some tools on hand that could assess data quality by scanning records and fields to check for uniformity of values. For example, a zip code could only be a five digit number, or a five digit number separated from a four digit number with a hyphen. If the scanning software found a zip code field that lacked either, or included some other value, it would be flagged. The data quality report Earl was staring at now showed him an alarming number of red flags. He was sorry he'd been so correct about poor data quality.

He decided that one way to deal with the address validation and credit score issues was to bring in a 3rd party data source as a clean reference. By comparing different data stores to this information, the developers would be able to determine which credit scores were correct, bring them into line with the scoring system rather than the letter grade system, and determine which address information was correct. This solution only solved part of the problem.

A major issue popped up during a limited test conversion Earl had conducted. Rather than looking at data quality across all of the systems that needed to be migrated, he had a small team run a limited conversion test. The test moved data replicated from the high speed Internet services customer database and one of the voice services customer databases through a conversion process into the new customer data hub's test environment. High speed internet and voice were among the first services that would be moved to the new platform. Charlie had won over the VPs who ran these groups, so they were willing to cooperate.

As Earl looked at the test report, however, he saw that the ratio of rejected to accepted records was nearly 3 to 1. Customer records still weren't matching up correctly. Even if many of the address and credit score fields had been rectified, there were too many records hanging. Everything from spelling errors to conflicting customer status – active versus cancelled – were creating problems. Earl realized that in the mass conversion, he'd be dealing with tens of millions of records overall, and millions that would need hands-on analysis and scrubbing.

Earl clicked on the dashboard he used to update the risk status of various projects and set the customer data migration to red. He then fired off an email to Jim Taylor that read

Jimmy-
Check your dashboard. We have a bigger data problem than you thought.
- Campbell

Within minutes Taylor replied.

"What did you do now?
I'm in Miller's office – stop by.
- Jim

Campbell walked around to the opposite end of the floor and into Miller's office past the Sherpa. Taylor was scrolling through emails on his Blackberry with one hand while typing a status report into his PC with the other.

"I'm not kidding Jimmy. We've got a real problem with data accuracy that could impact the whole migration plan and set us back a few months. This thing goes deeper than you and Miller guessed."

"And what does the risk plan say about contingencies here? I know we attended to that…wait, guessed? We didn't guess…"

"You're darn right you guys guessed. You were dead wrong in your first assessment. The contingency says we need to provide for additional time, resources and funds to clean the data. But you're talking about millions of records. That's a whole project unto itself. I actually think a lot of this will need to be scrubbed manually. I don't think we can create a new project team for this right now. We don't have the budget to hire new folks for this or to add it to ITSI's plate. We're going to have to be creative. Whatever options we think up probably have to go to the steering committee."

"Nuts…" Taylor exclaimed.

"Exactly mastermind, that's why I came to you."

"Alright Earl…This isn't entirely unanticipated and clearly it's a priority. We'll find some budget somewhere to get this done."

"Can I make a suggestion? I mean an actual suggestion."

"Please."

"If we stick with the risk plan, we can go to that partner in India that's doing some of the interface work for us to connect the biller with the customer data hub. They could probably help us here."

"But the budget…"

"No, I know that. Your buddies from ITSI Consulting are doing good work, but they don't work cheap. Maybe we can get the folks in India to do the technical part of the migration for us, plus all the cleansing and prep work, for about the same as what we budgeted for ITSI to do the migration. If we can put an option like that in front of the committee, we have a chance of getting it through I'd think."

"Good thought. That's a distinct possibility. But tell me this - what would sending this offshore do to us from a risk perspective? Did we account for that? I think the committee will get its knickers in a twist about sending customer information out of house, and off shore to boot."

"Yeah, we need to flesh out a security plan and put some guarantees in the contract about how they handle things on their site. It introduces some new risks for us, but I think they're manageable. Obviously we need to coordinate the folks here that are installing the apps with the guys in India who work on the data. There are timing and commitment issues we'll also need in the contract, especially since we'll need to fast track this. But, I'll get those into the plan. I'll work with you on some *realistic* contingencies on the technical side. The security issue will be a little touchy, but I don't see that we have much choice."

"We'll let the committee make that call. For once Earl you don't sound like a raving lunatic!"

"Yeah well, don't get used to it. And don't forget to tell Marc that this is all his fault. Dowd is going to blow a gasket when he hears about this."

Dos and Don'ts for Chapter 6	
DO:	**DON'T:**
Identify risks first, and then determine how to mitigate them.	Be closed to innovative new ways of sharing risk and rewards with vendors.
When deliverables are early or late, understand the root cause.	Assume your ideal end state is realistic given the current state of the architecture and the time and money available.
Have architectural standards that take the existing environment into account.	Feed your analysis with hearsay and opinion instead of hard facts.
Gather your facts, and then perform your analysis.	

For more information on how EMC Consulting can assist you with your transformation visit: - **www.emc.com/services**

CHAPTER 7

It was the first week in August and Michael Kim listened to the early morning call with interest. He planned not to intervene unless asked to do so. At the moment, he was letting Charlie Dowd do his job and admired his willingness to make a key vendor take on risk in order to protect his own budget. Mr. Kim, the name Earl Campbell and Pat Morton decided to tease him with, was not one of Charlie Dowd's guys. His job was to monitor budget issues, keep an eye on the program's costs, and report back to CFO Langdon Willis regularly. Though Dowd had specifically requested a member of the finance group be assigned to the program to promote financial visibility to the CFO's office, Kim knew he was ultimately an outsider, even in a group that didn't treat him that way. His responsibility was to the CFO.

Kim was a CPA who'd worked primarily for major accounting firms before joining Unidigitel. His goal was to become a professional CFO and he considered himself fortunate to learn from a veteran like Willis. When Willis' reputation was tarnished as a result of Brad Forrester's incompetence, Kim took it personally. So when Lang called him into a one on one meeting to explain his new assignment, to oversee Charlie Dowd's program, he recognized that he had earned his mentor's ultimate trust and had an opportunity to help mend his reputation.

"Can you explain to me how this conversation happened between you and Mr. Dowd?" Kim asked curiously.

"You know, it's funny, because Charlie surprised me," Willis told him.

"How's that?"

"Well, I knew from when I interviewed him before that he was a stand up guy. But I went into the discussion convinced that this was a run away program no matter who took it over. So, I have to give Dowd some credit because he shifted my thinking a bit. He said a few things up front that got me listening. First, he knows the program was too fat to begin with and that Forrester's answer to missing deadlines was to throw money at contractors. Dowd's guys scaled things down right off the bat, so that was a good start."

"You're saying he's a business guy who knows tech, not another techie who wants to buy expensive toys."

"At the least, yes. He told me that he's 'betting his job' and that he needs our help 'to keep things reined in.' Then he insisted that I put someone on his team because he planned to review the budget every week, publish his financials monthly, report to the board on where things are in relation to the business plan – really open the whole kimono."

"So this is not an overly political guy either, just a little dramatic."

"Funny you mention that, because he even said that if he got into trouble, I'd be the first person he'd call after Liz. That's why I called you in here. I don't want to take those 3 a.m. calls."

"Of course not…"

"The thing you need to look at Michael is how his team has rewritten the program's business case. You'll see they're trying to streamline things so we can bundle and do customer service instead of product service. They want to compete in the market, not in the science fair, so it looks very different from what you saw with Forrester. Dowd is doing a solid job of getting the business owners involved too. You should attend his workshops. He says they 'reduce the mystique.' I think he's trying to show everyone he's cooperative and fully accountable, but not afraid to push back hard to keep the scope in check. We'll see if he follows through."

"Lang, if I may, I'd like to make sure the audit committee is involved with this. I've looked at the report they produced before Dowd came on board, and it was frightening. I'd like to get an idea of where we are today in relation to that report and make sure we're taking care of some of those issues."

"Dowd told me he wants a monthly audit review of what his folks are doing. That's what surprised me the most. It's what he ought to do, but I am surprised, and maybe even a little wary. He plans to have his people deliver weekly updates to the audit committee. I want you to stay in sync with those updates and make sure they're delivered."

Kim knew the audit updates would be necessary to show how effectively Dowd's team was righting the ship. As Forrester gave way to Dowd, the audit team had done a complete review of the program and rated it as the "worst of the worst." Forrester had missed on deliverables, let the scope of the program get away from him, and as a result of both, costs overruns were rampant. As deadlines were missed, Forrester had continued to hire contractors in order to catch up and try to make up for mistakes he didn't want to admit. All of this was relatively well known to the committee before its audit began. What surprised them was that core elements of any program were missing. There was no realistic risk plan, no test plan, and no plan for managing vendors. Requirements hadn't been signed off on and there was no formal process for reviewing requirements changes, reporting budget status, or for escalating issues to a senior committee.

When Dowd brought Marc Miller and Jim Taylor on board, their first job had been to attack this laundry list of issues and put the necessary structures in place. When Michael Kim was assigned to the team in early August, he'd begun working closely with Miller and Taylor, helping to refine many of the processes relating to scope and budget that were most relevant to the CFO's office. Charlie made it clear to Michael that he himself wanted to be responsible for any change order that would add $10,000 or more to the spend. Kim respected the level of accountability he was trying to drive into the program.

Kim would communicate directly from the program office to the audit committee. The weekly reports were formalized, but it was his regular communication and insight that put the progress in context for the committee members. Early on, Charlie had set an expectation that given the depth of the issues that needed to be addressed, the fixes couldn't all happen overnight.

"We want to knock off these issues as fast as we can," Charlie had told Kim, "and you should make sure the audit committee understands the effort involved and what the results are as they emerge." Kim understood was that Dowd was asking him, if not explicitly, to help Lang Willis appreciate the investments and risks. Dowd wanted Lang to understand that while some work might appear cryptic, it would be backed up with a legitimate business case and signed off on by himself or Miller before it could move forward.

Many of the senior business owners, and the CFO himself, had little faith in IT after Forrester's failure. Dowd wanted to make sure everyone understood the business value and financial impact of every activity the program conducted. "Look," Dowd had told Kim, "we all know that any scope creep will kill this project. That's why I'm putting this containment strategy in place. If we back that up with tight budget management and keep everyone aware of what we're doing and why, we'll keep that nasty old genie in the bottle."

Though Michael could do without the metaphors, he understood Charlie's point. The reason Kim was on his team, and needed to be something of an outsider, is that he was a symbol of the openness, oversight, communication and accountability Dowd wanted to enforce. Being something of a neutral third party, he gave Dowd extra credibility.

Michael Kim began working with Marc Miller, Jim Taylor, and Earl Campbell at the point where they'd largely redefined the program's end state architecture. Reducing the scope and budget was somewhat simple at first because Miller knew that all of Forrester's undocumented skunk works projects would be cut outright. Teams of contractors and vendors that were working on proofs of concept that had no tangible use were ended to stop the program from bleeding cash. Forrester had been testing experimental network components, interactive video systems, and other technologies that wouldn't be ready for prime time for several years. There was no immediate business case to justify these efforts so they were stopped as a matter of policy.

As far as Michael Kim was concerned, reducing and revising the budget was only one step towards financial sanity. The program needed to define specific financial metrics by which Kim could measure budget compliance, track specific budget components, and understand costs related to technology, productivity, and personnel. Tracking specific numbers on a project by project basis, and then aggregating them up to the program level, would allow him to stay ahead of any cost issues and respond to requirements changes – and emergencies – from finance's perspective. Jim Taylor asked him to provide a list of the specific metrics he wanted reported on a monthly basis and Kim was more than willing to comply.

Having generated a spreadsheet to share with Taylor, Michael composed an email to make his recommendations official. It read:

Jim-

Attached is a spreadsheet with the financial metrics you requested. I've been impressed thus far with your focus on status reporting, problem detection, and knowledge documentation. I would hope, and expect, that you'd apply the same energy to these metrics to ensure that the project teams report them regularly and accurately.

Best Regards,
Michael

The attached spreadsheet included a detailed list of metrics that Taylor could distribute to the project leaders and on which Kim expected them to report at least monthly, and in sync with any notable changes.

Financial Metrics

FIMT Candidate Metrics for Solution Delivery

Sample Financial Metrics For Ed		
Area	**Family**	**Metric**
Financial	Budget Compliance	Project Budget Compliance – Actual
Financial	Budget Compliance	Project Budget Compliance – Forecast
Financial	Budget Tracking	Project Spend – Monthly Actual
Financial	Budget Tracking	Project Spend – Monthly Budget
Financial	Budget Tracking	Project Spend – Monthly Variance – Actual
Financial	Budget Tracking	Project Spend – Monthly Variance – Actual Percentage
Financial	Budget Tracking	Project Spend – Project Variance – Actual
Financial	Budget Tracking	Project Spend – Project Variance – Actual Percentage
Financial	Budget Tracking	Project Spend – Project Variance – Forecast
Financial	Budget Tracking	Project Spend – Project Variance – Forecast Percentage
Financial	Budget Tracking	Project Spend – YTD Actual
Financial	Budget Tracking	Project Spend – YTD Budget
Financial	Budget Tracking	Project Spend – YTD Variance – Actual
Financial	Budget Tracking	Project Spend – YTD Variance – Actual Percentage

CONSOLIDATED METRICS TABLE

Later that day, Jim responded to Michael with an attachment of his own.

Michael-

Thanks for the metrics sheet. There were no surprises there. Take a look at what I've attached here. This is a template from my playbook that I'd like to use. I'll have the project managers track all of your metrics, but we can use this template to aggregate their reports and provide you with a clear status dashboard for where each project stands in the program timeline and what its financial health looks like. I will get the numbers inserted within the week. Hopefully you and Mr. Willis will find this useful.

Thanks again,

Jim

The template Taylor sent would be useful, Kim thought as he examined it. It would act as a dashboard to keep track of the connection between the metrics reports he received and where the program stood in terms of development and milestones. As the newest member of the program team, he'd been skeptical about the group's willingness to be open with him, despite Charlie Dowd's assurances. Jim Taylor had just showed him that he was willing to back up Charlie's words and would at least attempt to support Michael's financial oversight role.

Status Template  UNIDIGITEL

#	RYG	Name	Description	Phase	Comment	New Dev & Carry Over	Current Project Estimate	YTD Actuals	Deliv. Date
1		PMO Discovery	Discovery effort for Program re-set	Complete	Discovery phase completed pending final report				July/Q3
2		PMO Dashboards	PMO tools for status monitoring	Final Testing	Existing tools reconfigured and nearing roll-out to PMO team				July/Q3
3		Project Reporting	Project team tools for docs & reporting	Final Testing	Existing tools reconfigured and nearing roll-out to project teams				July/Q3
4		Commapps Billing	New Billing Implementation	Initiated	Business reqs underway; Technical reqs being rewritten				NYQ1
6		CustVue CRM Elim.	Old CRM Decommission/De-integrate	Suspended	Project suspended pending final decision on CRM solution				TBD
7		Commapps Prod Cat	New Product Catalog Implementation	Initiated	Business reqs underway; Technical reqs underway				NYQ1
8		MasterDat Hub	Customer Data Hub Implementation	Initiated	Implementation progressing; New business reqs being defined				NYQ1
9		Web Portal	Web Portal Development, Implementation	Initiated	Requirements definition progressing				NYQ1
10		Analytics Engine	Customer analytics implementation	Pending	Pre-requirements being evaluated				NYQ1
11		Prod Data Cleanse	Product data cleansing and prep	Pending	Pending data quality evaluation				Q4
12		Cust Data Cleanse	Customer data cleansing and prep	Pending	Pending data quality evaluation				Q4
13		Prod Data Migrate	Product data migration	Pending	Scheduled to initiate Q4				Ongoing
14		Cust Data Migrate	Customer data migration	Pending	Scheduled to initiate Q4				Ongoing
15		Integration Bus	Integration bus implementation	Pending	Pending final decision regarding bus replacement				Q4
16		Bill-Hub Integration	Billing to Customer Data Hub Integration	Pending	Pending bus decision				NYQ1
17		Portal Integration	Web portal integration to bus	Pending	Pending bus decision				NYQ1
18		AMO	Adoption Mgmt Office Tools	Initiated	AMO structure defined and initiated by ITSI				Aug/Q3
19		UAT	User Acceptance Testing	Pending	Schedule to initiate Q1 next year				Q1-ongoing

STATUS TEMPLATE TABLE

His next priority would be to work with Earl Campbell to understand the cost implications relating to the changes in the architecture that were being proposed. He had a feeling that his interactions and exchanges with Campbell wouldn't be quite as simple, or as pleasant, as his communication with Jim Taylor had been.

The incompatibility between the billing platform and the CRM component Forrester had spent millions to customize and test remained a sticking point. Al Marcus was pushing to use Commapps' pre-integrated CRM. Earl Campbell wanted to run with Al's idea outright, but Kim had to assert his perspective.

"Earl, you realize that you're talking about a $20 million write off. That includes the work that's already been done, outstanding invoices Forrester had been hiding, and the buy-out clause in the vendor's contract. That'll go to the audit and steering committees. It could go to the Board. Lang won't just back this. Someone will be held accountable for it. Is that you?"

"Mr. Kim, I was thinking that Bradley already took the fall for that one. He was canned because of stuff like this. I'd argue that we'll save ourselves $20 million or more by cutting it now."

"You need to explain that so everyone upstairs understands how you can justify this move and how much it'll save in the long run."

"This is one of those 'amputate the leg to save the soldier' situations. There isn't another choice that makes sense in the long term," Campbell said.

"I get that. They won't," Kim replied. "They're looking at next quarter. They don't want to hear a bunch of mumbo-jumbo about how the customer data lives in this hub over here, while CRM and billing stuff live over there. It took me a few days to understand it myself. Charlie will have about 15 minutes to explain it to them. You'll have to turn this into an elevator pitch or it won't fly."

Campbell swore under his breath, but knew Kim was right. "Alright. So, let me ask you – how do you recommend I make that pitch?"

"The tech piece is up to you. But I'd say you'll have to make it clear that this was probably Forrester's biggest mistake with the architecture and that the only way we can fix it is to bring in Commapps' component. You'll have to explain how we do this without getting bent over in the process on the new CRM piece. If this advances the time to revenue on this program by a full quarter, show them how. But, like I said, they need to understand how much it would cost to follow through on Forrester's plan versus how much it will cost to replace it."

"I'm guessing it'll free up about 20 contractors. It'll cut out three or four months of integration code and testing…"

"Make a list, put the dollar amounts next to it, and I'll take it to Lang from there. Does that work for you?"

"It does. I'll get you those numbers by the end of the week."

During the last week in August, Rod Bender waddled uninvited into Miller's office. He had become a particular thorn for the team, and Michael Kim was getting ready to lock horns with him. As long as Bender talked schedules and requirements, it wasn't Kim's place to step up. But when he began creating issues that impacted the budget and the program's timeline, Kim was poised to push back.

"I'm not just going along with this nonsense," Bender said to Miller, Al Marcus, and Michael Kim. "I won't support another endless CRM program."

Bender did have a point. He was responsible for sales and as such was under increasing pressure given how much ground had been lost in the past year. He was angry that Forrester fed him promises about new sales force capabilities that he failed to deliver.

"I've had some teams working with 'sales-funnel.com' and I see no reason not to put all of my teams on it. It works. It's simple. And people learn it quickly. I have numbers to make this quarter and I don't need my senior people doing systems design for you. I need them selling."

"Rod," Miller replied patiently, "we looked at that option already. It's not a long term solution. It's not going to support the bundling you need to do."

"Well Marc, I'll remind you that I have my own budget to put toward this. I don't need to run down a rabbit hole with you. And I certainly am not cooperating if my recommendations are just going to be ignored," Bender retorted.

"Your budget is approved by our office Rod," Michael Kim seized the opening aggressively. "You're bluffing, even if you don't know it. Lang isn't going to sign-off on any parallel projects that don't tie into this program. So you need to get on board here and stop trying to bully Mr. Miller. It's in your best interest to play ball. This whole program is geared to put big dollars in your pocket in the next three years. Make enough noise and you might draw the kind of attention you don't want. Last time I checked, we were losing customers."

Al Marcus stepped in to play the mediator. "Let's all calm down for a minute," he said. "Rod, I think it would be best if you brought your concerns to the table formally so we can address them for you," Al said in his most welcoming tone. "Maybe if my folks showed you the application, or brought you on-site to an installation, you'd have a better vision of what it can deliver. Brian Walker made a similar request. We'll be happy to bring both of you out to a reference site if you'd like."

Bender knew he was trapped. If he refused Marcus' offer, he would be exposed for playing politics. He also knew Kim was right. He hadn't fully calculated the wisdom of Charlie's move to have him join his team until that very moment. The CFO's office didn't just control the program's purse strings, it controlled everyone's. Lang might have been skeptical, but Dowd had been smart enough to convince him that this program was critical to the business and that streamlining it and containing IT costs and effort across the board was necessary for success. Bender wasn't ready to give in just yet, but for all of his blustering, he was experienced enough to recognize when he was on unsteady ground.

"I'll have my assistant contact you about dates for that on-site Al. I'll take a look at your system, but that doesn't mean I'm convinced you guys will deliver anything. My head's on the chopping block here too and I'm not letting a bunch of engineers submarine another year for me."

Bender turned quickly, and ungracefully, and shuffled out the door.

"Nicely played fellas," Marc Miller said to Al and Michael. "I think Rod might have realized for a nanosecond there that he's not as clever as he thinks he is."

In October, the DRM component issue surfaced. Taro Kawaguchi, who led wireless sales, was pushing back against the program team, following Bender's resistant lead. Bender had little choice but to accept that the new CRM component was being geared to suit his teams. But that didn't mean he would go out of his way to make things easy on Charlie Dowd, Marc Miller and company. Michael Kim could see that the DRM problem could become a new battle that might escalate to the executive steering committee. He didn't hesitate to bring Lang Willis up to speed to try to head it off.

"Michael, good morning," Willis said. The large wrap around windows in the room gave a clear view of the hills surrounding Unidigitel's campus and Kim always liked to stop for a moment to take in the view. "What's the word today?"

"Morning Lang," Kim said breaking his gaze from a hilltop in the distance to look his mentor in the eye. "I just wanted to give you the heads up on an issue that'll be coming your way pretty soon."

"Sounds interesting."

"It's a bit technical, but it impacts the budget and there's some conflict with the wireless folks. I suspect it'll end up in front of the executive committee. There's this function called DRM, it stands for digital rights management."

"I'm somewhat familiar with that Michael. It has something to do with protecting movies and music from being copied."

"That's right, but in this case it's a bit more complicated. Part of what we're trying to do here, to get ahead of the market a bit, is to let anyone with our video recording service grab their recordings from their set top box and watch them on their mobile."

"That makes sense. What's the problem?"

"Well, we need to bring in a new component to make it happen. There's some work to do to find the money for it in the budget. I think the program's reserve will cover it, but I'm still analyzing it. The real problem is the wireless group. They have a DRM component now that helps protect music downloads, but it won't support this content sharing that's one of the main goals for the whole show. The program team wants a central DRM system for everything. The wireless guys, Taro in particular, want nothing to do with it. They say it's not going to work exactly the way they were told originally, but Charlie assures me that it ultimately will. He's building it in phases because it's a new technology and he doesn't want to risk spending a lot to customize it if it he doesn't need to. The wireless guys are running promotions for the next three months to drive their content sales and they don't want any disruptions to their DRM system or any of their people pulled away to help with new requirements."

"How soon does Charlie want to replace what they've got?"

"Well, that's the thing. His team won't be ready to test it for another four months anyway. So it won't really interrupt the promotions. Mostly they're being difficult for the sake of being difficult. But, the way we operate now is that we don't push forward with things like this unless the business owner signs off on it. We can't even get their requirements in the mix because they refuse to cooperate with Charlie's guys. This could end up on the steering committee's agenda later this week. I wanted to make sure you understand the costs, the impact to the timeline, and what everyone's issues are."

Michael reviewed the costs and budget options with Willis for 20 minutes. Together they determined that some of the dollars could come from the IT reserve budget that had been set aside, and that a transaction-based, pay-as-you-go deal could be negotiated with Commapps to amortize the cost and push much of it back to the production phase.

Lang then turned to Michael and said, "I think we'll need to back Charlie on this issue with the wireless group."

"I think its Charlie's job to…"

"Granted. But I know Kawaguchi and I know Bender lets him get away with anything he wants. Taro has always produced the best sales numbers in this company, which is why he's still here even though most of us think he's arrogant. At this point, I think we know that Charlie isn't looking to make power plays. He's trying to do the right thing. He needs to make his deadlines. He needs this piece to do what Liz, and frankly Bender, ultimately want. And he knows he can cut some cost out of the picture by consolidating things, which he's trying to do here. Taro, on the other hand, is all about power plays. He may have some legitimate hesitations about IT getting in the way of his sales teams, but I suspect he's just trying to see how far he can push things. I think it's time to put him in his place."

In early January, Kim walked into the first audit meeting of the New Year and was surprised at the attendance. All such, meetings were open to all of the program's stakeholders. There were more business and functional owners in the room this day than there had yet been at previous meetings. Michael wasn't sure whether this meant people were buying in to Charlie's approach, or if they were hoping to see the new CIO and his folks get their clocks cleaned. If the latter was the case, they'd be disappointed.

"As you know, your original report on this program included a list of nearly 100 issues to address rapidly, many of which relate to program structure and related processes," Jim Taylor told the committee, addressing Lila Green, the chairwoman, directly as Charlie had suggested. "If you'll look at this next slide," he advanced his presentation, "you'll see that we've tackled most of the major issues."

Taylor's slide included a table summarizing items he'd emailed to the committee members in a spreadsheet several days before. The team had developed a new structure for the program covering everything from issue escalation and requirements management to schedules, sign offs, revised risk plans, budget updates and more. The executive steering committee was on board and detailed requirements sessions had been conducted with business owners and their key SMEs. The program was moving forward and wasn't bleeding cash at the rate it had just six months earlier.

The major issue, the one that kept Jim, Miller, and Charlie up at night, was the relative lack of tangible results. Most of the effort thus far had gone into putting the program structure in place; re-designing the architecture; dealing with a long and

Issues

Project Issue - Details

Project Name		NuView CRM						
Project Manager		Ted Alexander						
Request No	Link to Project Issue Document	Issue Description and Impact to Project	Priority (HML)	Reported By	Status	Date Assigned	Assigned to	
NV-CRM-09	http://unid/lib/0034	Test Environment Hardware. Potential 90 day delay	H	D. Smith	Red	12/01/08	T. Alexander	
NV-CRM-19	http://unid/lib/0103	Schedule Requirements Baseline Workshop. Must be scheduled in next week to avoid impact.	H	A. Johnson	Yellow	12/02/08	T. Alexander	
NV-CRM-25	http://unid/lib/0154	Sufficient CRM Module Expertise. Potential Configuration Delay	H	D. Smith	Yellow	01/05/09	A. Marcus	
NV-CRM-35	http://unid/lib/0178	Latest CRM Build from Commapps	H	T. Lucas	Green	1/15/08	H. Chang	

ISSUES

aging issue log; collecting requirements; putting out fires; and performing development and integration work. None of the new, front line applications were live yet. None of the efficiencies promised had been realized yet. And while the team knew that the early returns were just three or four months away, they also knew that everyone that wasn't part of their core team was wary about IT's ability to deliver anything useful.

As Taylor gave his presentation, some folks in the room seemed disappointed at the lack of carnage. Some heads were nodding around the room, particularly among the committee members. They could see Charlie's people were effective. As the meeting wrapped up, Green's closing statement summed up the majority opinion in the room. "We're not quite there yet, but we're certainly seeing major improvements. If we stay on this track, I think we'll see the deadlines made and the budget under control. But let's remember that we need to see all of this work deliver something useful to the bottom line. That's what the Board expects and they are impatient. Charlie set a high bar for himself and they know the program is already at least a month behind. I want to see you succeed, but I'd suggest that you focus more on some more tangible benefits. You'll need to make a strong case to the Board for why this program should continue through the rest of your roadmap."

Dos and Don'ts for Chapter 7	
DO:	**DON'T:**
Have support from functional groups like the CFO's organization and the audit committee.	Let vendors skate.
Promote open project reviews and deal with the good, bad, and ugly.	Be afraid to call out errors and stop the bleeding, rather than taking a "hope springs eternal" approach.
Know the scope and budget.	Let people miss deadlines, blow budgets and walk on.
Track actual budget progress weekly.	
Take accountability for road bumps, but stop the bleeding.	
Use trending to show progress.	
Explain the benefits in financial terms to the CFO, Board and business owners.	
Drive accountability by assigning people to the right jobs and aligning the different jobs.	
Make sure people do what they are supposed to do so you can call them out fairly if they don't, and applaud them when they do.	

For more information on how EMC Consulting can assist you with your transformation visit: - **www.emc.com/services**

CHAPTER 8

With just days left before the 90-day Board review, and after all of the budgetary drama involved in cutting the old CRM project, neither Charlie nor Miller relished their next task. No one liked breaking it to a vendor's account manager that he was losing the major account he'd worked for as much as 18 months. This was part of the dirty work that came with righting a sinking program.

"I understand, and I'm not entirely surprised," Rick Williams said in his basso voice. The 6'4" former college basketball player from Illinois had an intimidating presence, but ultimately he was a friendly and cordial man who understood the value in never burning a bridge. "This whole project has been burning for a while, so I figured there was at best a 50/50 chance that either we'd be out or the guys from Commapps would be. When I heard you brought Al Marcus to town, I figured it would be us."

"Well, you should know that we have no intention of disputing the termination clause in the contract. We'd like to make this a clean break, legally speaking. But, there are some personnel who've been working on your solution we'd like to keep in the fold," Miller told him.

Terminating this contract would be painful. Lang Willis had accepted it only begrudgingly, and only behind closed doors. He'd opposed it publicly with vitriol Charlie knew wasn't entirely feigned. The out clause required Unidigitel to pay CustVue a $8 million fee for termination. But hacking the partially installed CRM component off like a gangrenous limb would mean writing off another $10 million or so of work that was already done. Miller had determined that maybe $5 million worth of investment would be salvaged in the form of process definitions, requirements development, and data identification.

Willis was only convinced to go along because Miller demonstrated that Unidigitel would save at least $20 million on the custom integration, development and long term maintenance work that would have been necessary to integrate CustVue's CRM component. Miller knew there was a substantial risk that the integration would run over budget and throw off the entire delivery schedule. This was a primary reason the decision was made to use Commapps' CRM component instead.

"I think my superiors will at least be glad to know this isn't going to get any uglier than it needs to, and I think we can come to terms on some consulting fees for keeping some of our folks on board to help you through the transition. I can also tell you that you'll see me around." Williams said the last with the hint of a smile. "It wouldn't be the first time we saw Commapps struggle a bit with their solution."

Charlie read the subtext of this statement immediately. What Williams was really saying was, "if and when you fail a year from now, I'll be poised to take this account back." He was tempted to tell Williams not to bother, but instead gave Williams an especially firm handshake that said "you don't intimidate me" and "don't bet on it." Charlie Dowd didn't like having to break the news, but he wouldn't lose any sleep over it either. Williams wasn't the problem. He knew he'd cashed in a big chip with Lang Willis that would give him and his team much less wiggle room in the coming months.

In early September, with the Board review behind them, it was time to hold a critical meeting that would define the transition from Forrester to Charlie Dowd. The program team met with all of the vendor team leaders and project managers who would remain involved in the program. Though many of the people in this meeting were aware of the changes that had been taking place under the new leadership, this official gathering would set the tone for the program as it moved forward.

The team would unveil the new architecture, having received the Board's blessing, and introduce the new protocols and metrics by which the program would be governed and measured. Charlie and Miller had discussed the fact that after this meeting, each vendor had to understand what its responsibilities were, where the boundaries of its domain lay, what milestones had to be reached to trigger payments and bonuses, and that each player's compensation was dependent on everyone making deadlines.

Charlie wanted to make sure that everyone got the message that teamwork was not just important, but necessary. Further, everyone – including his own people – would be measured according to a well defined set of metrics by a neutral group of folks from ITSI Consulting who would be responsible specifically for vendor management.

At the beginning of this day long meeting, which would be held in one of the large ballrooms at a local hotel conference center, Miller and Jim Taylor reviewed the new architectural plan and laid out its redefined scope.

"We've made massive changes in the scope of the program and have simplified things to make it easier for all of you to understand the progression of activities, your specific deliverables, and the dependencies among each of the individual projects," Miller explained to the 37 managers in attendance. "I want us all to understand that as far as this program is concerned, we're all on the same team and we all ultimately report to Charlie Dowd. We all have to work according to the same rules regardless of which company we thought we worked for before this meeting," he said. There were murmurs of confusion and subtle dissent throughout the ballroom.

"Now, the upside to this…" heads turned back in Miller's direction, "for all of you is that we'll succeed this way. I know a lot of you have been frustrated at the lack of progress for the past year. We're going to change that. We've simplified the scope of the program to make sure we have reasonable goals at each step. But I can't stress enough that individual successes aren't enough. We have to succeed as a team, and that's why my bonus, and Jim's, and frankly Charlie's are as dependent on all of you making your deadlines as your own bonuses and payments are."

"We're not trying to punish anyone," Jim added. "We're all putting our money where our mouths are and we all depend on each other."

A number of heads nodded in affirmation around the room, though the general mood remained one of curiosity and some skepticism.

"I'm sure you're all wondering what's changed about the scope and schedule." Miller continued. "For starters, our year one goals have been sharpened. We need to get the new multi-service and cross-network offerings up and running. We want to have new customers who we will target initially, and who come to us to take up the new offerings, managed in the new customer data hub. That component needs to be in production by April 1st next year."

Murmurs and gasps ran across the room as realization set in that Miller had just announced an aggressive, seven month launch deadline.

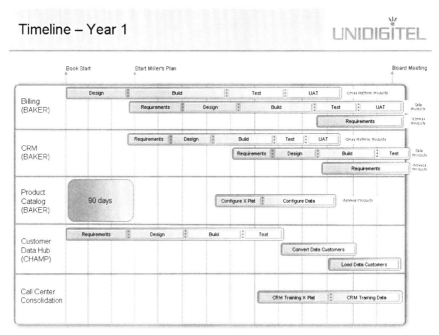

TIMELINE – YEAR 1

"We'd like to have our on-shore call centers merged by the end of next year. Another critical piece this year will be to set the stage for a bigger data migration in year two. We'll need to spend significant time on data analysis, cleansing and transformation. We're planning to move all customer data into the hub and all product data into Commapps' product catalog. Which brings us to the architectural changes. Jim?"

Jim Taylor stepped forward and summarized the architectural shift.

"That should put the dates Marc just announced into some context. What this means for all of you is many fewer moving parts, and many fewer dependencies. This should make it much easier for everyone to make deadlines and earn those bonuses."

The sense of relief in the room was palpable, though the schedule remained aggressive. Miller and Taylor hoped the managers could see that they were being set up to succeed, not pinned down with wholly unrealistic expectations with no chance to earn the bonuses they'd been offered.

"Jim, do you mind if I add something?" Miller asked.

"Go ahead," Taylor replied.

"Probably the biggest challenge we'll bite off in this first year is getting the customer data hub into production and set up to support our contact center consolidations. That will require some significant integration work between the hub and the billing platform. There are some templates for interfacing the two, but we need to be able to support specific processes that will change over time, making the interfaces between these systems a significant risk area."

A hand shot up in the audience from one of the members of MasterDat's team. Miller paused to receive his question.

"Who's taking on that integration? Is that also the billing guys? The SI?"

"Good question," Miller replied. "I was just getting there. We've been impressed with work we've seen your offshore group do on this kind of integration. The billing teams will have their hands full with bringing their product catalog and CRM pieces online, so we'll turn to your folks in Bangalore for this interface development. Al Marcus says he's had success working with them in the past so this made sense to us. Do you have any objections there?"

"I probably would have suggested the same thing," the questioner replied. "Our subsidiary over there does great work on interface development and data migration. Who's handling the migration piece?"

"We're still in discovery mode and assessing all of the data quality," Miller replied. "We'd like to have ITSI Consulting handle that piece with some of the folks from your team and from Commapps. We'll keep that in-house. But part of the reason we want your folks to do the interface development is so that if we did need to turn to them for help with moving the data, they'll already be in sync with us. As a matter of fact, that's a contingency in our risk plan."

More heads began to nod as if to say, "this guy is organized. We can get behind this." Miller's reasoning, which he didn't voice to the group, was that he liked MasterDat's offshore team because it was a subsidiary and not a partner. He'd felt the pure partnership models – or 'papership' as they were often dubbed – weren't effective. Further, from a risk perspective, he didn't want to put absolutely everything in Commapps' hands. It made sense to spread the risks around.

After a break for a catered lunch of fresh sandwiches, cold drinks and snacks, Miller and Jim reviewed the new program structure, escalation procedures, the steering committee's role and contributions, and change management processes. Most of the managers were already familiar with the new requirements gathering process. They had participated in various workshops already with representatives from the different business units.

Jim Taylor then asked everyone in the room to stand up and find a new seat.

"This isn't one of those 'get to know your neighbors' ploys. I can see some folks struggling with the post-lunch food coma, so let's all move around a bit and wake up." Chuckles rippled across the room as Taylor put everyone at ease with his collegial and light hearted approach to running what could otherwise be interminably dull meetings.

Once everyone was reseated, Jim and Miller covered what was expected of each group in terms of documentation, archiving project artifacts, procedures for budget approvals and changes, status reporting expectations, and the purpose of the new and far more detailed risk plan. The vendor personnel and contractors had to adopt, embrace and adhere to the structure and governance Miller and Jim had designed. They had already experienced Jim's continuous demands for documentation and status reporting and were familiar with the tools he'd made available to them, such as the monthly update sheets the managers had dubbed "Jamaica Reports" because of their green, yellow, and red sections used to indicate project budget, schedule, scope and quality statuses.

Monthly Status Report   UNIDIGITEL

Project Monthly Status Report

Project Name	NuView
Prepared by:	Jim Taylor
Date (MM/DD/YY)	09/07/08
Reporting Period	09/01/08 – 09/07/08

1. Executive Summary

Overall Status

	Green	Yellow	Red	Reason for Deviation
Budget	[]	[X]	[]	[Re-Architetcure]
Schedule	[X]	[]	[]	[]
Scope	[X]	[]	[]	[]
Quality	[X]	[]	[]	[]

1.	Process is within budget, scope, and quality
2.	Process has deviated slightly from the plan but should recover
3.	Process has fallen significantly behind schedule, is foreseen to be significantly over budget, and has gone beyond the original scope

Comments:	Program generally in Green Status. Budget overruns have been caused by need to close down original CRM project and vendor.

MONTHLY STATUS REPORT

147

As the meeting progressed it became apparent that everyone in the room appreciated the new leadership and organization Miller and Taylor brought. Morale was improving and even Earl Campbell could see reason for some new found optimism. A sense of urgency was permeating the group. The schedule was extremely aggressive, but for once everyone knew what they had to accomplish and how they were to go about working within the program.

Because Charlie Dowd had taken it upon himself to reengage with the business owners and earn their buy-in, he had to sell Brian Walker, SVP of customer care and support, on a plan for shelving but replacing his data warehouse project. Walker had proven to be a good ally thus far, largely because he wanted input into the look and feel of the new web portals Charlie was building for his agents. But Charlie knew that Walker had his own agenda and had to be handled delicately.

Walker was infuriated when he learned indirectly that Forrester had no chance of making the deadlines that would enable him to drive his call center consolidation. Walker had budget and performance goals he wanted to meet and hated that they depended on what he saw as an incompetent and wasteful IT organization. By mid-October he had been running his own data warehousing project for months. He was determined to show that he could take matters into his own hands and achieve what his colleagues in IT had not. Even with Charlie's team making rapid progress, Walker chose to continue his project as a hedge against anything that might delay IT's ambitious program. When Charlie approached him, Walker was resistant to any suggestion of changing his plans.

"Brian, I think you need to take a look at what we're doing before you reject what I'm saying," Charlie implored him.

"Charlie, look, with all due respect, I think you have enough on your plate that you don't need to worry about my little project over here. I have my own deadlines I want to make. I'm just not going to let my stuff take a back seat to billing or to whatever it is that Bender might want from you. My people are running this thing just fine, so just let it go."

"I think you're forgetting that I'm not the program manager Brian. I'm responsible for every piece of IT we put into this company, no matter who manages it." Charlie didn't really want to pull rank, but he was frustrated with Walker's brash attitude. "Your folks are doing a good job, but a stand alone data warehouse goes against everything we're trying to do. So why don't you tell me what it is that you need, and I'll come back to you with a plan for how we deliver it."

"I'm no more than three months away from having this thing finished, so I don't see how your people are going to lap me when your production deadline is in April…"

"I do. Your people have done a ton of work in redesigning your processes to migrate all of your product support and sales into two streams – consumer and SMB. That's aligned with what we want to do. You've also identified the data you need to get things moving in that direction and you're planning to replicate it and stuff into this data warehouse. Am I wrong?"

Walker didn't respond right away. Charlie was correct, and Walker realized that Charlie wasn't eating lunch in the cafeteria just to ingratiate himself to the troops. He'd been collecting intelligence, and he was good at it.

"You've done your homework. Go on," Walker said flatly.

"I'm hoping you'll have your project team become a part of our program." Charlie could just order him to do it and have Willis cut off his budget, but he wanted to try to catch this fly with honey before resorting to the flyswatter. "We'll adopt your requirements. The work you've already done on cleansing some of the product data will help accelerate our billing implementation. And I want your process folks to help the CRM team to move forward faster. Miller and I discussed this. We can commit to meeting your phase one goals within four months and giving your supervisors first crack at the alpha-version of the new tools. You can benefit from them while you help us test them. How's that?"

"What happens if you don't make it?"

"For starters, no one on my side gets their bonuses."

Walker raised an eyebrow. "Okay, but what about my call centers."

"We'll deliver weekly status reports to you. If anything goes yellow, we'll pull resources off other projects to make sure we deliver what you need on time. I just need you to support what we're doing."

Walker realized Charlie was sticking his neck out for him when he could easily pull rank and end the argument. "I need to talk to my guys before I agree to anything. What you're offering is fair, but my people were cheated by IT before and might not be as open minded to this approach as you'd like. Can you ask Miller to reach out to my project manager today or tomorrow? I'm sure my guys will have a load of questions and details to work out. So, I'm agreeing with you in principle, but I'll get you an official answer within a week."

"That'll do. We'll make this work Brian. Stick with me."

Ground Hog's day had just passed and the yellow status that stared at Earl Campbell as he popped open his dashboard only added to his worsening mood.

"Son of a…" he swore under his breath. Yet again the customer data problem was rearing its ugly head. The project team responsible for the customer data hub implementation was falling behind schedule. The group in Bangalore to which the data scrubbing had been outsourced was stretched thin. Its interface development work had suffered due to the added workload and was now more than two weeks behind.

The on-shore team had only just received the news and reported it upstream. That team consisted of subject matter experts and a project manager from within Unidigitel, several data modeling and migration experts from ITSI, and three product experts from MasterDat. The project manager's report, which Campbell was now reviewing, suggested that the problem would likely set the team back three weeks or more. This once again put the launch in jeopardy, as well as everyone's bonuses, at a time when there was no longer any room for error. That interface needed to go into beta-testing in just less then two months, and February is a short month.

Earl brought the issue to Miller's attention on Thursday evening, February 5th, and the two agreed to make it a primary discussion point for a team call the following day.

"We need a real assessment of the work this interface needs done to get back on schedule. Michael also needs to know what happens to the budget if we need more hands," Charlie stated, though everyone on the call had anticipated his points.

"The guys in India know their side of the interface – the data hub side – real well. They fell behind because they're learning more about the billing side of the interface on the fly than we realized. We were under duress when we sent it out to them, so I'm not sure how well we vetted their people. It was a trade off to spare the budget, if you'll recall," Campbell explained.

"I think the issue Charlie," Miller responded, "is that if we pull people off of other parts of this project at this stage, we might impact the timing of other pieces of the launch because we're running so lean as it is. It's all starting to come together now, so there's less wiggle room. I think we need to keep that risk in mind."

"Marc, I'm disappointed in you," Al Marcus quipped. "My team is about two weeks ahead of schedule – and I know you're aware of that. I can spare some of my 'A' people who know our side of the interface to pull the development over the finish line. We can also offer up the test environment we established for the product catalog data and order process to speed up the testing once the interface development is done. There's very little cost to do that. I think my guys can get this back on schedule. They'll gloat about it since you took this piece of the project away from them. But they'll do it." Al knew his team would go for it. If the data hub fell behind, his team could miss dependent milestones that would hit them in the pocket. None of them wanted that to happen. They might not be happy about reaching out to help the other vendor's project team, but they'd certainly be motivated to bring it back on schedule.

"Al, I'll ask you to work with Earl and Jim to push that forward this week," Charlie said, impressed with Al's willingness to step up. "I'd hope that by our call next Monday we'll know whether the schedule will be affected. I don't need to remind you that if it's bumped back any further, we're all on the line for it." Charlie closed the issue and moved on with the early morning call.

When Al's team communicated with the developers in India to coordinate their efforts, they received some good news. They had fallen behind, but had been doing quality work. Their side of the interface was stable. They'd laid out more than 80 percent of the mapping between the two systems and had done it cleanly. Al's team was able to play a consultative role that helped to accelerate the process. With the teams split between California and India, it meant late nights for Al's guys all through the weekend, but it also provided the advantage of an almost 24 hour work schedule.

The teams had nearly seven work days worth of work done in three actual days. The people in India would produce documents and write code that the team in California could review, test and debug. Results and change requests were in the developers' hands in India by the following morning. The collaboration was effective and the timing was an unforeseen but not surprising benefit of Campbell's original risk mitigation strategy.

The 7 a.m. call on the forthcoming Monday was more upbeat than anyone had expected.

"This, my friends, is why we have a risk plan," Jim Taylor said.

"I'd like to take credit for this," Campbell responded, "but I have to admit that I didn't completely see this coming. I probably should have, but I was a bit distracted. I gotta give Al credit for pulling this through."

"That's generous of you Earl, but I'd be lying if I didn't

admit that it was my team that did the work, and they did it because they want to trigger their bonuses, like everyone else."

"This my friends," Miller quipped, "is why we set up the compensation structure the way we did. Al, I have to say thanks to your guys for donning the Superman cape. Your folks are doing a heck of job."

"You're welcome Marc," Marcus replied."

"Enough with the black slapping guys," Charlie stepped in. "It's not done yet. They've made good progress. If they can keep it up for another week, will we be back on schedule?"

"That's what it looks like," Al answered. "But I'll keep a special eye on this piece and make sure it's done right for you."

"Good," Charlie said. "Let's not lose focus. We've still got the whole launch to make. I don't want us celebrating because we made a tackle on second down. Understood?"

There was no need for any reply. Miller broke the silence.

"Al, I'll see what I can do about some kind of extra little sweetener for the people from your team who tackled this for us. What pleases me here is that the program is functioning the way it ought to. We're a few weeks behind where we originally hoped to be because of the data issue in general. But I think we're now on a realistic schedule, we've shown we can maintain the pace, and we should have some tangible benefits to show by the time you go the Board Charlie."

"You all have my confidence," Charlie said. "I don't think we can rest, but I think we'll make it under the wire. Let's just stay on top of all the little issues in these next couple of months. Watch all the details folks."

Charlie wanted to keep his troops motivated and maintain the sense of urgency that had gotten them this far. They were doing an excellent job, but he was still concerned about the expectations he'd set with the Board and how soon afterward they had irretrievably fallen behind schedule. He hoped more than believed now that he'd have some tangible results to show by June 1st. Either way, he'd have to do some tap dancing to sell the Board on it even if the launch came off without a hitch and the new offerings made an impact in the market.

"Parma," Charlie continued, "you've been a bit quiet on user adoption. Let's get everyone up to speed on where you stand."

Dos and Don'ts for Chapter 8	
DO:	**DON'T:**
Know vendors' statements of work, timeframes, and deliverables.	Allow vendors to move outside of their defined scope unknowingly or invade other vendors' areas.
Have deliverables, not a runaway train.	Allow vendors to replace A-teams with less qualified people without permission.
Optimize vendors' resources and skills.	Automatically blame vendors when things go wrong.
Know their chain of command.	Derail vendors with poor efinitions or poor change management processes.
Exchange services: Do speaking engagements, visit development sites, etc.	
Tie bonuses and payments to deliverables, milestones, and deadlines.	
Have vendors share in the pain and costs as needed.	

For more information on how EMC Consulting can assist you with your transformation visit: - **www.emc.com/services**

CHAPTER 9

Parma Singh, within a few weeks of having regular working sessions with Charlie, Al, and Jim, and leaning on Earl to understand the aspects of the changing architecture had come up with an action plan for herself. First, she had Jim help her pull a small team of experts from ITSI Consulting together to help her form an adoption management office or AMO. This office would operate from within the PMO. It would be responsible for managing the entire adoption management lifecycle from definition and design in the early phases through development, testing, and deployment, and ultimately to maintenance and ongoing improvement of the new solutions.

"I think it makes sense to launch an internal marketing campaign so that all of the impacted user communities understand what's going to change, how it will benefit them, and how they're voices can be heard as we go through the various development, testing and adoption phases," Parma told Charlie during one of their regular work sessions.

Charlie liked Parma right away. While she was extremely tentative and quiet during their first meeting, he could see she was becoming comfortable with him and was willing to state her plans rather than ask permission for them. She had management skills. She was organized, smart, attentive to detail, and a good communicator when she decided to assert herself. He had approached her as a mentor and coach. He encouraged her and helped her work her way through her own decisions. As a result, she came to trust him and knew she would be able to ask for his help without making herself vulnerable to ridicule or undermining his confidence in her.

"What did you have in mind?" he asked her, genuinely wanting to understand her vision.

"Well, I've read quite a bit on this subject, but I think some of my sources didn't take into account all of the tools we have available," she said. "They encourage us to establish a brand that user's can relate to, and I've given that some thought. But they also talk about using posters and banners to promote positive messages around that brand. I don't think those things are useless, but I want to create a community for all of our users."

Charlie was intrigued. Part of the reason Charlie wanted someone younger and a bit more in touch with the front line groups was just for these sorts of non-traditional ideas.

"I read the audit reports and the survey HR conducted in regards to morale in the user community," Parma continued. "Put simply, it's rather poor. I want to do something that will inform and energize these people."

"Makes sense," Charlie replied.

"I was thinking that we should establish a private group on Facebook where people can learn about what's happening, share their ideas and complaints, and feel like they're part of the process. I would encourage the focus groups, as they try out the new tools, to use Twitter so they can share their reactions – good or bad – with the group."

Charlie frowned, but Parma had anticipated his concern about security and his lack of familiarity with these sites.

"We can link those comments right to the Facebook page, which is invite-only, and I can control who follows and views the Tweets. We can use the group page to collect and respond to comments and show that we're listening. Even if we can't make everyone happy, I think we will gain a lot of support if we just give everyone a voice and make them feel that they're being heard and having a positive impact on the program."

"I think those are good ideas," Charlie told her encouragingly, "but I would like to see some more detail and make sure corporate communications is in the loop before we kick that off. Okay?"

"Of course, I understand." She knew he was still concerned about security and couldn't quite envision what she had in mind, but she was determined to show him how it could work.

"I think," Charlie added, "that you should encourage the focus groups to hold their own meetings with their peers so they can communicate the good and bad. Overall you want to get people excited that the new systems will make their jobs easier and give them more tools for creating promotions, selling new services, or make people happy by solving their problems more quickly. I think face to face meetings shouldn't be replaced by all the social media stuff you're talking about."

"I don't disagree, Mr. Dowd," she said. "But consider that the different groups you've referenced, or even the various contact center staffs, are all in different places. I'd like these people to communicate across the geographies in ways they never have before. I also would like to cut across organizations so those face to face meetings include people who, for example, work on this campus and yet have never met."

Charlie frowned in thought and for a moment Parma thought he hated the idea. She was wrong.

"That's actually really smart Parma…I never would have looked at it that way."

"Well, I've done quite a bit of reading about this," she said. "And I use some of these things to keep in touch with my brothers in India and my friends in the U.K. But, a friend of mine was telling me recently that her company has started to use a community approach like this for problem solving. She said she'd been trading messages with three other people for two months when they finally realized they all worked in the same building but had never actually met before. That's essentially where I got the idea."

"What did you have in mind for the brand name?"

"I had my first meeting with some of the middle managers from marketing, from the local call center here on campus, a few product managers who could make it, and some of the billing folks. We brainstormed and took a vote. It was actually quite fun."

"And what did you come up with?"

"We want to call it New View…but spelled "N – u – V – i – e- w." We played with YouView, like YouTube, and with things like Customer Center and even 'Easy Button.' In the end though, the managers thought that NuView explained what we were trying to deliver and that we could wrap it into all kinds of slogans. They'd like to run with it. Do you have any objections?"

"You know Parma, this is your turf. You don't need my approval on that. If you think it'll resonate, and you'd know better than I would, and the managers chose it….Well, I trust that you'll make it work."

"Thank you Mr. Dowd. I believe we will."

Parma was committed to having regular meetings with the middle managers from marketing, sales, customer care, product management and billing. She believed that openly communicating with them in the early stages through a series of open workshops was the only way to gather the right user interface requirements, maintain consensus, and take a realistic and reasoned approach to change management. These were the people who had come up through the ranks and knew the existing systems, processes, and roles and responsibilities best.

She also knew that engaging these people was the only way to break through the kind of resistance and disconnection that often made IT programs fail in adoption. Even if the IT groups made their deadlines, the software could be dead on arrival if the users rejected it. She also knew they had to understand what the systems could and couldn't do for them so that they could develop realistic requirements.

Another major reason she needed to have a trusted relationship with these managers is that she had to ask them to lend her some of their best people for an extended period of time. The program needed experienced and smart people from each of these areas to comprise the focus groups. These would be central to refining requirements and testing the new solutions. They'd also have to communicate progress to their peers who were still using the old systems and help through the coming transition to NuView.

When Parma explained the focus groups to the managers in mid-October, she received mixed reactions. Several of them had already lost some of their best people to burn out. Some had been cherry picked by headhunters, and others had been laid off. A few of the managers were newly promoted and were hesitant to exercise their authority and assign colleagues, who were friends and recently hierarchical equals, to new responsibilities. But some of the managers got it, and they proved useful allies for Parma.

"I think what you need to understand," Bill Rice, one of the more seasoned managers from the care organization told the group, "is that it's a good career opportunity for these people to be named to a focus group. They get to influence the direction of the new tools, and they're the ones who teach everyone else how to use them in the end. You have to sell it that way."

"Well then why can't some of us assign ourselves to the focus group and leave our folks in their jobs?" one of the newer managers suggested.

"Don't be naïve," Rice fired back, "you need to manage your group through all of this. Whoever you assign to the focus group will be a lieutenant for you, to help you get your whole team through the transition."

"Just a moment," Parma stepped in. "Now, Bill is correct that the managers need to manage. But there's no need to argue here. I'll give you detailed information about the kinds of skill sets and experience levels we need across the focus groups. That should make it easier for you to narrow down who you'd want to assign and give you some breathing room. We need different types of people to make this realistic. If someone absolutely does not want to participate, I'm not sure we'd want them in a focus group anyway. But again, Bill is correct in saying this is a great career opportunity."

This seemed fair enough to most of the managers. But when Parma received their assignees a few days later, she found that some of the managers had chosen people that just weren't qualified. One of the culprits was a sales manager from the wireless unit. He had been quiet in her stakeholder meetings and she knew him to be a disciple of Taro Kawaguchi and Rod Bender.

Parma had sent him a text message saying:

"Let's talk. Not sure you get what we need for focus group."

"I'm sorry Parma, but I can't spare anyone else," he told her after she tracked him down in a hallway the next day. "We're heading into the holiday season and I need my best guys selling."

Parma had tried reason and was prepared to pull the escalation card.

"Let me make this easier for you," Parma told him firmly. "There's a process in place for dealing with this. If you and I can't resolve this together, it gets escalated to Mr. Miller. Then Mr. Miller calls your boss, Mr. Kawaguchi. I suspect that won't go well. In that case, the issue would escalate to the executive steering committee at which point Mr. Dowd will bring it up to Mr. Bender. At some point, you'd get a call from Mr. Bender and he won't be very happy with you."

Parma was bluffing a bit. She knew something this trivial was unlikely to be escalated that far, but she wanted to make it clear that someone who could make this person's life unpleasant would see him as a squeaky wheel and intervene.

"Are you threatening me?" he asked.

"Not at all. I'm just explaining how the escalation process would work. Why don't we just make this easy on ourselves? The problem with the people you've recommended is simply that they are inexperienced. Neither has been with the company for more than three months. If you don't want to spare your best sales people, I can understand that. What the project calls for is someone who's been around long enough to understand your systems and processes and could use some time off the front lines. Tell that person they have a chance to get paid and recharge without the pressure of making quotas and dealing with complaints in the retail centers. If we can identify that person, we can solve this problem without it going upstream."

"Fine," the resistant sales manager replied begrudgingly. "I think I know who you need. But let's just say you'll owe me a favor for this."

"Fair enough," Parma said, wondering what she might be getting herself into. "I'm willing to owe you one. It'll only make things better for both of us if we can work this out ourselves."

Parma's inherent need for organization made measurements and metrics central to her management style. As a project manager, she often measured progress amongst her teams at a level more granular than her managers even asked. Working in Forrester's program had been maddening to her because reporting was almost non-existent. His program failed to capture meaningful measurements and utterly lacked the structure needed to put any useful measurements to good use. Working with Miller and Jim was a relief because they believed in tracking and reporting detailed metrics.

Late one night Parma reviewed documents her team members from ITSI had forwarded to her. She crafted an email to Jim Taylor seeking his help in defining the measurements most important to her role in adoption management.

Mr. Taylor -

I've been through nearly 100 slides relating to adoption management techniques and aggregated what I think is most important into the attached. Can you help me to take these measurements from the general to the specific? I could use your guidance here.

Thank you,
Parma

She attached her new slide to the email and sent it off before turning in for the night.

Measurements and Metrics:
Four Key Elements of Adoption

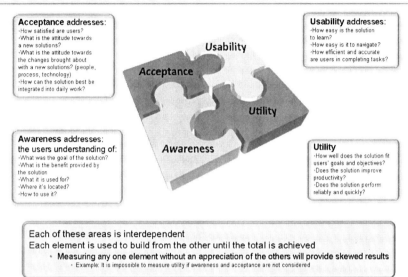

Acceptance addresses:
· How satisfied are users?
· What is the attitude towards a new solutions?
· What is the attitude towards the changes brought about with a new solutions? (people, process, technology)
· How can the solution best be integrated into daily work?

Usability addresses:
· How easy is the solution to learn?
· How easy is it to navigate?
· How efficient and accurate are users in completing tasks?

Awareness addresses: the users understanding of:
· What was the goal of the solution?
· What is the benefit provided by the solution
· What it is used for?
· Where it's located?
· How to use it?

Utility
· How well does the solution fit users' goals and objectives?
· Does the solution improve productivity?
· Does the solution perform reliably and quickly?

Each of these areas is interdependent
Each element is used to build from the other until the total is achieved
· Measuring any one element without an appreciation of the others will provide skewed results
· Example: It is impossible to measure utility if awareness and acceptance are not considered

MEASUREMENTS AND METRICS: FOUR KEY ELEMENTS OF ADOPTION

The next morning, Parma found a reply from Jim in her inbox.

Parma-

I think you might be struggling here because some of these measurements are a bit softer than you're used to in more technical projects.

For the contact centers and retail stores, you can measure things like how long it takes to resolve issues, how many clicks it takes to complete certain processes as compared to the legacy process, how many screens someone has to look at to fulfill an order, fill out a trouble ticket, or answer certain types of common questions. And of course how many calls or emails someone can handle in an hour, or whatever time frame you think makes sense.

I think the softer stuff always takes more creativity. You probably want to get your focus groups involved early on.

Expect these things to evolve over time too. It'll be tough to measure user performance or support calls early on, but when you start testing, you might want two groups. You make one group do everything with the new system and observe where they struggle and turn to the documentation most often. The other group can work side-by-side with the systems they're accustomed to, and you can track where they choose to turn back to those systems to get over the hump in certain processes. This is observational, so you need some folks to step outside the group and track their colleagues. You'll get a good read on which issues are universal, which are tied to certain individuals, and which don't improve with system familiarity and can be tracked back to bad flows in the UIs or bad performance on the back end.

Also, surveys are always good, especially if you can get people when they're fresh off a test and still riled up about it. You might also want to look at benchmarking this against other companies that have done similar projects before. Go ahead and reach out to Dawn Casella or Chuck MacLaren from ITSI on this. I think those guys can guide you the right way on this stuff. That's what we're paying them for!

Regards,
Jim

Parma knew this was good advice. She had become so accustomed to doing things hands-on and for herself that she probably wasn't leveraging all of the resources she had available to her. She decided to reach out to Dawn and Chuck and have them put a plan together, as Jim suggested, so she could focus on running the AMO and keeping the major efforts aligned and moving forward.

"I know you're all convinced you know what's best," Charlie told the group of senior business owners he was addressing. He'd been holding regular status meetings with them throughout the requirements phase. As development pro-gressed and process re-engineering became more of a reality, the meetings had become more engaged and heated than in the early stages.

"I'm not trying to tell you that you don't know your busi-ness. What I'm saying is that you don't realize how constrained you were by the old environments. We have an opportunity to make you more efficient and even better at what you do. Remember the three-legged stool I've been talking about: peo-ple, process, and systems. I need you to forget about how things have worked and how your old systems constrained you. Let's talk about how you want your processes to flow and what you want your people to focus on," Charlie told them.

"Right Charlie, but you've been telling us all along that the system likes to do things in certain ways," the head of product management pushed back. "So we can tell you what we want, and then you tell us why you can't do it that way."

"That's not accurate," Al Marcus interjected. "What he's telling you is that you have an opportunity to make massive improvements. Sometimes your visions are the right way to do it. Sometimes, we can look at the ultimate purpose behind your ideas and show you a proven way to accomplish it that we've got pre-developed in a solution asset. Why reinvent it if we can show you how the best players in the world in each area became the best?"

The room erupted in a chorus of, "malarkey" and "of course the product guy's going to say that" and others saying, "hey, listen to what he's saying! It makes sense if you just pay attention champ."

Al glanced at Charlie as if to say, "well, I'm trying," and Charlie stepped forward. He'd had enough of the cacophony. "Enough everybody! Listen. You're looking at things from your individual perspectives. We're going for enterprise-wide improvements here. Let's stop wasting time and look to the guys who've succeeded at this before."

No one moved. There was silence in the room as every-one absorbed Charlie's unexpected outburst.

"Good, so we all agree on that. Here's the deal, some of the stuff you're asking for isn't aligned with the overall goals of simplifying operations, achieving customer-centricity, and pulling the product offerings together. If you don't get something exactly the way you asked for it, that's most likely going to be why. The reason we're having these meetings is to work together and figure those things out so I don't have to dictate them to you. This is a workshop. If you want it to be a fight, we can get ropes and gloves and do it the old fashioned way," Charlie said the last with a grin. The tension in the room eased off. Charlie added - "Al here was an amateur champ back in England though, so I don't recommend it."

Al threw Charlie a perplexed sidelong glance. He'd never thrown a punch at anything but a piece of drywall in his life. Charlie shrugged and continued.

"What we need to nail down is how we merge your processes together. I'm working directly with Parma Singh on my team to run our AMO. Its job is to get your people involved in how we make these changes and to help them through the transition. But if that's going to work, then I need each of you to be in touch with your own folks and reinforce what comes out of these meetings so they hear the same things from you that they get from the AMO."

People in the room began to settle down and listen. Charlie was making sense. Most of them were accustomed to Forrester doing things in his own world and dropping bombs on them out of nowhere. Charlie knew this was why they weren't always willing to listen. By soliciting their input and including them in the process, he was slowly earning their buy-in, despite occasional resistance.

"Al and I want to understand your ideal visions for how your processes should work. We'll get you 80 percent or more of what you want, but you have to recognize that we're not starting with a clean slate. There have to be compromises. But believe me that Al and his team are the best in the world at this. You know what I did to get him here?"

Al had heard rumors about this story, but hadn't actually heard Charlie admit to it.

"One of his bosses is an Army guy. He owed me $1000 because my Midshipmen have kicked the Cadet's rears into the dirt a few years running. I cashed that debt in to get Al here."

You had to hand it to Charlie, Al thought to himself. He knew how to seize the attention of a room full of hard-nosed, type-A managers; keep them on their heels; and get them focused. Now Al had to live up to his reputation and the expectations Charlie had set for him.

"You tell us what you want," Charlie said, "and Al here can show you the best way to do it."

It was mid-November by the time Parma was the first to speak up on the 7 a.m. call. "I have an issue I'm going to need help with," she said to open the meeting.

"What's up?" Miller asked her.

"About a month ago I cornered one of the sales managers from the wireless group. Essentially, I told him that he needed to get in line or there would be problems."

There were several chuckles on the line, but Parma wasn't sure who had laughed.

"He agreed to cooperate," she continued, "but told me I owed him a favor. Without giving it much thought, I agreed. Now he's trying to call in that favor. He, a few of the other sales managers on his level, and now Mr. Kawaguchi are asking for a special console that will allow them to compare and beat price plans from the other major wireless carriers. It's not so much that I think this is a terrible idea, but it's in a vacuum. It's not within the scope we've defined. And it wouldn't take bundling into account. I could see this as something we would perhaps deliver in year three, but I've told them it can't happen now. They won't take 'no' for an answer."

"You know, it's interesting that you mention this Parma," Charlie said. "I have an email here on my Blackberry from Liz Fagan asking me why the wireless sales guys are bombarding her with complaints that we're not treating them fairly. Let me respond and see if she's online. I'll tell her our version of the story."

The other members of the program team chit-chatted for a couple of minutes. Charlie's Blackberry buzzed with Liz's reply. Fagan was known for almost always being accessible by mobile in the early morning hours. Charlie read her message out loud. It said:

Understood. I'll get back to you on this, but have your guys handle it diplomatically. Give the wireless guys two options you can live with so they feel they have some kind of choice and I'll make sure they pipe down.

"I'll tell you what Parma," Miller chimed in. "Jim and I will take this one. We know you've had issues with these guys before. We don't want you getting sucked into this trap. You have better things to focus on. We've got some items in the roadmap that tackle price comparison that we can sate them with, or their other issues can take a back seat. We'll settle this so you can carry on."

"Thank you Mr. Miller. That's much appreciated."

"Do it cleanly Marc. Liz asked us to be diplomatic," Charlie urged him.

"That's why I'm going to let Jim do the talking," Miller retorted sarcastically. "No worries Charlie, we have a few ways we can tackle this without upsetting our plans. We're on it."

Coming out of what had been a mostly productive workshop session in mid-January, Charlie pulled Al into his office for a quick chat.

"Al, I think these guys are starting to listen, but we still need one of them to help bring it around for us. I was thinking about hitting up Brian Walker for another favor, but I need to know if what I want to offer him is feasible."

"He's the outspoken one who runs the contact centers, yeah?" Al asked.

"That's right. He's sort of obsessed with collapsing all of our consumer-facing call centers and giving the CSRs tools that'll let them support and up-sell any product. He wants to get rid of the labyrinth of IVRs we have now and break industry records for time-to-resolution, and other metrics like that. He's even got an empty space on a shelf in his office for the award he's planning to win."

"That's optimistic," Al replied with a snicker. "But what's your question Charlie?"

"I need to know if it's realistic for me to have Miller accelerate the CRM project so we can prioritize this uber-CSR interface for Walker's supervisors. I want to offer him this in exchange for selling the other business owners, Al Bender in particular, on our ability to over-deliver for them. I think if we do that, we can bring them all into the fold. But I know Walker, I'm going to need to give something like this to get him on board."

"Well to be frank, I don't think the issue is with our product. The latest version, the one we're bringing in here, was redesigned to do exactly what you're talking about. I think the real issue is on the data side. We need the product and customer data pulled together to make it happen."

"So, we're back to the data quality problem."

"Yes. But, that said, we did something like this in Singapore where we federated a data subset. It was real customer and product data, but it only applied to high value customers in a limited geography. It was enough though to show the power of the application. I think that's what you really need. There's been enough work done on the test data and likely on the data scrubbing we sent to Bangalore, that we might be able to run with a similar approach. If we can use the test data as a source for now, and see what the guys in Bangalore can deliver, I think we can put something exciting in front of Walker."

"You mean, he could be more excitable? I'm not sure I want to see that," Charlie quipped.

"Right," Al replied coolly. "I think we can deliver something is my point."

After confirming with Miller, Jim, and Earl that Al's plan to put a sexy mock-up on Walker's desk using the cleansed test data would work, Charlie found Brian Walker on instant messenger and opened a chat to him.

Charlie: Brian, you got a second?

Charlie waited for a response. It came quickly.

Brian: What can I do for you?

Charlie: I've got an offer for you. I need you to back me up in the business owner workshops and help me sell this process to the other folks, especially Bender and some of the marketing guys. I can offer you something special in return.

Brian: I'm listening. Sounds interesting.

Charlie: Within three weeks I can put your uber-CSR UI on your desk and roll out a testable version to your top supervisors. It'll run off a limited data set, so it's mostly a mock up, but it'll meet the vision you have for your call centers. We can use this as an example of where we're trying to take everyone's consoles, and I'll credit you with being the idea guy and the impetus behind this.

Brian: That's good. I am that guy Charlie. If you're saying you'll step on the gas on my stuff in exchange for selling everyone else on your program, it's a deal. You kind of owe this to me for canning my data warehouse, but if this is what it takes to get you back to my original schedule, then I'm in.

Charlie: Deal. Always nice doing business with you Mr. Walker.

Brian: Likewise Mr. Dowd. See you at the next workshop.

At the next gathering, Walker was true to his word. Wisely, he didn't oversell it at first. He bided his time, steering the more resistant people with whom he had some influence toward Charlie's way of thinking. A month into the process, in mid-February, after two bi-weekly meetings, Walker had his mocked-up uber-desktop and began showing it to the others. It went over well. With visibility across each customer's entire portfolio, the marketing and sales folks began to see the potential of what the new architecture would mean for them.

The billing folks weren't tied to the UIs as much, but Al had been working them. By reputation, they already knew the performance improvements they could expect from the new system. Their bill runs would be accelerated and performance was already far better because Miller had canned the 3rd party ESB project they'd resented from the start. Al, however, had been showing them reports from previous projects that not only helped organize promotions, discounts, and price plans, but gave analytics on how different plans and packages performed so they could weed out the weak links.

Throughout the workshops with the business owners in January and February, Al had begun to flash more of his experience. He could draw on examples from nearly every major telecom player on the planet. If there was a product that was dominating a market and the industry news somewhere, Al seemed to have had a hand in it. Charlie facilitated the discussion and got the managers from different groups engaging each other in break out groups.

As the business owners warmed up, they talked about ways to drive efficiencies by eliminating redundancies in their groups. Some had epiphanies as they realized they shared many of the same frustrations. Charlie could see their attitudes start to shift. Instead of competing with each other, they could drive each other's businesses. They could make each other's products more compelling. They could make it easier to get products into the market. They could keep more of the customers they won because of the billing accuracy and care visibility they'd never had before but always wanted.

With Walker's encouragement, the more resistant business owners began turning to Al for ideas. Rod Bender, ever the squeaky wheel, had thrown every scenario he could think of at Marcus to try and stump him. Al met him at every turn. He'd take on the challenge by showing the whole group how he could take what the most advanced telecoms in Hong

Kong, South Korea and other leading edge markets were doing to dominate their competition and make it work for them. After a while, Bender was no longer challenging – he was engaged. He was smart enough to see that Al Marcus' stuff could make him rich. Charlie stood back and let it happen. Al wasn't just living up to expectations, he had exceeded them.

By mid-March the alpha versions of several of the new systems were being introduced to Parma's focus groups. Leading up to this pre-release, her teams had worked closely with the developers to lay the groundwork for "field guides." These served as early user manuals for those testing and tri-aling the new systems. Some of the field guide material was drawn from the documentation Commapps provided. The new process and functional flows had to be scripted though to provide references for the focus groups and lay the groundwork for the general release.

While developing the field guides, Parma applied the metrics she had defined with the managers. These were critical to determine what aspects of the new UIs and process flows were intuitive and useful, and which needed the most rethinking and adjustment. There was an inherent relationship between the focus groups' ability to work with the field guides in order to understand the new systems and the measurement of how well they adapted to the new flows.

One of Parma's focus groups was based in the contact center on the main campus. This group of ten supervisor-level customer service agents was among the first to have the uber-CSR consoles on their desktops. They had all moved their workstations to a cluster in the very middle of the contact center where they were extremely visible. Above their heads was a banner that read "NuView Center of Excellence." It was their job to handle all calls relating to sales and support for certain customers who were looking to add to, asking support-related questions about, or had billing questions relating to multi-product bundles.

Ultimately, the members of this "center of excellence" team would return to their supervisory roles in different clusters around the contact center to help their individual teams through the transition to the new desktop interface. They were central to the development of the field guides and provided critical feedback to the IT teams who would tweak the new systems throughout several subsequent releases. It was up to these people to hold meetings with their peers from the groups who did not yet have access to the new systems to keep them in the loop on progress and what to expect when the new systems were released.

In addition to running meetings, the focus group members here, and in other call centers in various geographies, were among the most active on Parma's community, social media sites. Parma was also active on these sites and would respond directly to questions, compliments, and complaints about the systems and the new changes everyone anticipated. There was significant anxiety because of the forthcoming changes to the systems, and because some folks realized their jobs could be in jeopardy once the contact centers began to consolidate.

Parma would often stay up late at night to scroll through numerous Tweets and posts on the Facebook site. She would catch herself sitting at her kitchen table staring at her laptop for hours more than she'd intended responding to comments and trying to answer as many questions as she could. She would take notes on what she learned and boiled down the most common feedback to a few key points she planned to share with the program team on upcoming calls.

The good, generally speaking, was that the swivel-chair effect was eliminated. Having data and functionality in one place was making the focus group users far more efficient. They felt they were better able to focus on interacting with customers. Before, they had to search for information. Some would take notes on paper to keep track of data coming from different screens. They no longer had to use the alt-tab command to switch between applications just to answer common customer inquiries. The general consensus, as far as Parma could tell, was the users were optimistic that as the applications were further refined, this benefit would make their jobs simpler and more engaging.

Two common complaints stood out, however. One was that customer data was incomplete. The focus groups had access to most of the new product information in one place, but customer data was still being cleansed and migrated. It was difficult to determine whether it was accurate or incomplete. The test users that had access to the legacy systems would use them to double check whether their new consoles were telling the whole story.

This, unfortunately, brought the swivel chair effect back into play. Users who no longer had access to the legacy systems were sometimes blissfully unaware of any issues. But as they spoke to their colleagues, their confidence in the data was undermined and they'd sometimes lean around a partition to see if they could grab access to the legacy databases for a quick check.

Parma realized as she studied comments relating to these particular issues that there were problems with the access permissions. In some cases it was clear that customer data was missing from the new consoles. In many cases, however, the issue was that the uber-users for some reason didn't have access to information they needed. Parma realized the permissions just weren't configured correctly. There wasn't much she could do to accelerate the data cleansing – that issue had long since been hashed out. The permission issue, however, was something she could address.

Permissions were critical to the new systems architecture because all users – including online, customer self-serve users - would essentially use the same web-based interface. Different types of users would have different views, and tightly controlled access to appropriate data. At this stage, however, there was no reason to restrict access so tightly for the supervisory level focus-group members who weren't security threats. Even in the full roll out, they'd have access to more customer, product and billing information than just about anyone in the company.

It was already 2 a.m. when Parma came to this realization, but she signed into the program team's status tool to log the issue. Parma intended to use the tools Jim Taylor had put in place to her advantage. She created a jeopardy item, flagged the status of the UAT deliverables as "yellow – high priority" and entered notes to describe the problem as well as how and by when she wanted it fixed.

She then jumped back on the Facebook site to post an update to her community, letting them know she'd discovered this problem by reading their helpful comments and complaints and that she'd flagged it as an immediate priority. Her post was time stamped at 2:23 a.m. Pacific time. By 2:30 a.m. she already saw comments and Tweets from community members in India and eastern Europe complimenting her for deciphering the problem and thanking her for taking action. There were also a few disparaging remarks made about the IT developers, but Parma decided to let these slide. A little healthy rivalry was nothing to fear as long as it remained healthy.

In early April, after the first release of changes was added to the new systems, the program team began rolling the beta version of the software out to a wider audience. Their goal was to have a number of second level care agents ready to support the new product launches in the initial test markets. As a result, they were able to limit the volume of data that had to be converted and focus just on key geographies where new offers and pre-promotions were being pushed into the market. As the pre-promotions began circulating, call volume relating to them began to rise. The good news was the promotions were compelling and there were many questions rolling in about pricing, features, and availability.

Parma found through her metrics and her community site that the groups who were working with the new systems were a bit frustrated at their lack of fluency with the new functionality. Call times, or average hold time – AHT, was longer than the program team and Brian Walker wanted to see. Too many of the agents, who continued to have parallel access to their legacy applications, were turning to those applications when they got stuck, rather than turning to the field guides and supervisors for coaching. The field guide was still in document form and as it had grown was a bit difficult to search. Parma had an effort underway to make it accessible online in a searchable format, but with limited resources focused on other priorities, that effort was slow going. She had multiple text messages and emails from Walker saying things like –

Parma- I need you to wean our guys off the legacy stuff. Get them trained better or roll it all back to IT.

Parma knew he was frustrated and that there was no going back at this point. The issue was double edged. The good news was that the supervisors who had disbanded the initial focus groups and returned to their clusters, as planned, were highly fluent with the new systems. They were stepping in when trouble occurred, having other agents escalate calls to them when they were stuck. Those customers were responding positively. Surveys and reviews of recorded interactions showed that they felt cared for personally. They enjoyed the extra chit-chat with the care reps and felt those reps were going the distance on their behalf. Those calls were showing more successful up-sales of bundled items and add-on features. These were all positive signs.

The bad news was that too many calls were being escalated. The supervisors who'd been involved in the focus groups were playing the role of superhero rather than training their colleagues to work through their confusion and gain more familiarity with the new tools. AHT was rising because the supervisors would become backlogged during busy hours as the front line care reps were taking liberties with the escalation procedures.

Parma knew that action had to be taken but was wary of using Byzantine measures like shutting down the parallel systems or forbidding escalation to supervisors unless the customer specifically asked for it. Instead of making up new rules, she once again turned to Chuck MacLaren and Dawn Casella, her colleagues from ITSI, for examples of how they'd handled this kind of situation with other clients in driving better on-the-job training.

The problem for the front line users was that their training had been truncated late in the game in order to make launch deadlines. Charlie was under the gun with the critical, year one Board review fast approaching. He was already, in his opinion, 6 weeks behind where he'd told the Board he'd be at this point. He told the team time and again, "you have to deal with changing the tires on the truck while it's rolling down the highway. We just can't slow down."

The consequence was that the broader group of users who were pulled out of training to support the new service launches, though excited about the new tools, weren't comfortable enough yet to rely on them, even though they were simpler to use. Old habits die hard and there hadn't been sufficient time to break them. The good news was that the vast majority of users was still being trained and would have more time to acclimate. But Parma recognized that she would have to do more to measure their competency coming out of training to ensure this set of problems didn't repeat itself in the subsequent market launches.

It was decided that the new systems wouldn't be forced into the wireless retail centers until they were fully baked. Parma appreciated this decision. The wireless group had been a squeaky wheel all along. While they had become far more cooperative since their showdown with Miller and Jim, everyone knew they were waiting for an excuse to raise a fracas over any blip they could find. Rather than complicating the contact center conversion with a simultaneous conversion in the retail centers, they were given workarounds based on their existing point-of-sale systems that allowed them to promote bundle sales. Sales reps in the stores would call a particular, PIN-secured 800 number that would connect them automatically at the supervisory level.

A final problem Parma faced was with the online, self-help version of the sales and care interface. Some of the retail centers had kiosks installed where customers were given a "sneak peak" of the NuView self-help portal. A good number of customers jumped at the chance to try it out since they could search through phones, price plans, and bundle plans on simple menus without waiting in line at the counter. The bad news, Parma found in her online travels, was that while customers were posting and Tweeting about the new systems publicly, their remarks were often disparaging. She found and collected comments in a document like:

"Good info, but ugly as sin."

"My 4th grader could design a better looking site."

"Could they make the buttons any harder to click?"

This was the trade-off of going with Commapps' interface. It worked well from a functional standpoint. Aesthetically, however, it left a lot to be desired. It was still in a relatively early development phase. Parma began building a business case for investing in some simple look-and-feel, design improvements prior to the general release of the self-help tools. With this business case, she proposed leveraging the social media buzz around the product to turn the negative into a positive by addressing the issue directly and revealing plans for a design improvement based on the feedback from the public.

Parma's overall impression, despite the adoption challenges she was facing, was that people were engaged. The market was attracted to the new products and channels. The early signs, despite these anticipated bumps in the road, were positive. She just hoped they were enough to help Charlie through the Board review and keep the program alive long enough to deliver on all of its promises.

| Dos and Don'ts for Chapter 9 ||
DO:	DON'T:
Get the users involved early and often.	Overlook the need to have the whole user community - not just testers and focus groups - bought in.
Anticipate the re-engineering and training needed.	Forget documentation and field guides to make the transition easier.
Plan for all three legs of the stool: systems, process and organization or people.	Give new users too many opportunities to stick only with what they know.
Find creative ways to promote the benefits of change.	Leave training and transition management as an afterthought.
Gather and respond to feedback from users who will be impacted by coming changes.	Have people testing and trialing the systems who won't be primary users when they go live.
Measure user performance and progress at every step of the way.	

For more information on how EMC Consulting can assist you with your transformation visit: - **www.emc.com/services**

CHAPTER 10

"Don't you think that's a bit dramatic Marc? I don't think we're about to have our heads chopped off in this meeting," Charlie said to Miller reassuringly as the elevator ascended to the top floor.

"Then why have you tugged at your tie three times since I stepped in here?" Miller retorted.

"I think we're about two months behind where we wanted to be, where we'd said we'd be, by now."

"Well, we started in a pretty deep hole..."

"Right, deeper than I anticipated. That's what bothers me. I should have seen it early on. I should have set the expectations a bit more reasonably. I was too optimistic at the 90-day meeting and I ought to know better."

"I think you're being too tough on yourself chief. We've made a mountain of progress here..."

"Yeah, and we've spent a ton of money and cruised head-long into this mess of an economy we're in now. Those guys upstairs, they don't care if the program functions right. They don't care if we're making project deadlines and hitting milestones. They want results. They want to spend less and make more. They want us to leapfrog our competitors, especially CM&E and blow away their video bundle. They want to beat the lousy guidance they gave to the analysts. I think we'll get 'em there. But I have to do a heck of a sales job today to convince them we're turning the corner."

"We are turning the corner. The test markets we launched the new bundles and cross-network offerings in are showing huge wins. The personalization, the a la carte offerings, the content sharing – they're all winners. We *are* ahead of CM&E. We're at the top of the cost curve now. We're a few weeks away from the inflection point based on the numbers we're seeing. Sure, we've had a few setbacks, but if those guys in there aren't smart enough to understand that we're saving their ship, then they don't deserve to sit on that Board."

"Okay Marc. Why don't you tell *them* that?"

"No way man," Miller grinned devilishly, "that's your job."

Liz Fagan greeted Charlie and Miller as they stepped out of the elevator.

"Charles, Marc, good to see you." Liz liked to call Charlie by his proper first name. It denoted respect, but also implied the closeness of their relationship. No one else, other than his mother, ever called him Charles. Liz stepped forward as if to embrace him, clearly thought the better of it as her eyes quickly darted back and forth, and instead shook each man's hand firmly.

"How's the weather?" Charlie asked her, referring to the Board's general mood.

"Partly cloudy, chance of sunshine," she replied somewhat uncertainly. "Lang's in a surprisingly positive mood today. He seems to like you guys. Well, as much as he likes anyone anyway."

She turned and opened the tall, polished wood, double doors that allowed entry to the Board room. At the center of the room was the long, oval, enameled table surrounded by designer arm chairs that swiveled and adjusted in 12 directions. Several of the Board members were seated, while others mingled around the room chatting with their colleagues about business, golf, their political opinions, and the distressed economy.

A small LCD projector peeked out of an alcove in the ceiling and presented Charlie's introductory slide on a large, drop-down screen at the far end of the room. As the three entered, several of the people in the room stepped forward to greet Charlie and wish him well. Charlie wasn't certain which were genuine, and which secretly looked forward to lambasting. As he shook various hands and exchanged pleasantries, he moved to the head of the table to begin his presentation. Miller remained close to the door, on the far end of the room, ready to add any details should Charlie call on him to do so.

Charlie Board Agenda    UNIDIGITEL

- Overview
- Scope & Strategy
- Benefits
- Current State
- Risks and Issues
- Next Steps

CHARLIE BOARD AGENDA

"Good afternoon folks and thanks for coming," Charlie began. "As you know, we're here to review the progress we've made on the customer-centricity and web channel alignment program. I'll give you some background to refresh your memories on where we started and what our initial plans were. I'll then show you how we've progressed, where we are today with the architecture, and what this means to our top and bottom lines." Charlie paused to take a breath and make eye contact with various people around the table. Lang Willis gave him a slight nod of acknowledgement.

"I think it goes without saying that we need to discuss how the economy might impact our plans for the next year if we find our resources constrained. Before we do though, I want to talk about what dialing back this program could mean from both benefits realization and risk avoidance points of view." Heads nodded in acknowledgement, though several eyebrows were raised at the words "collective decision." What Charlie was doing, several of the Board members realized, was letting them know up front that he'd resist any notion of suspending or massively downsizing it. The program's end goals remained critical to Unidigitel's future and it was only just beginning to bear fruit. Charlie hit the button on the remote mouse to advance his slides.

Program State Of the Union

> **Mission:** Reset the NuView program. Deliver business value from investment.

> **Vision:** Establish viable program focused on execution and delivery.

> **Achievements:**
> - Re-planned, Built and executed a measurable new plan that has achieved benefits
> - Re-architected. Simplified, re-focused architecture
> - Re-resourced. Reduced number of vendors. Reengaged best resources. Restructured teams
> - Re-scoped Program. Reined in shadow projects
> - Provided program transparency and accountability
> - Reengaged business. Achieved business alignment

PROGRAM STATE OF THE UNION

"If you'll recall," Charlie continued, "the original purpose of this program was to restore Unidigitel to market leadership. We decided that a key to doing this was to drive all of our business activities and supporting operations in a customer-centric direction. A main objective was to consolidate much of our IT architecture and simplify our operating environment to reduce cost and risk. We also decided to align all of our web channels; improve customer interactions across sales, care, and support; and to enable as much self-service as possible in all of those areas." As Charlie looked around the room at this point, he could see recognition and acknowledgement in everyone's eyes.

"Additionally," he went on, "we want to establish common platforms and portals that would help our care unit to consolidate the call centers and drive cost out of the business. I've been working closely with Brian Walker throughout this program and can tell you that he's passionate about solving that particular challenge." No surprises, objections, or questions were yet evident.

"Now, you'll also recall that when you brought me here, this program had gone terribly astray. Without spending much time going over the history there, I want to put some of our achievements of the past year into context."

"We've had to put significant effort into restructuring the way IT and the NuView program operate. We had to build the support structure nearly from scratch to manage the program appropriately, re-engage the business owners, rein in the budget, and ensure that all program activities are completely aligned with our stated goals. We've consolidated many 'shadow organizations' across the business. These were IT projects that individual business units had launched because the former program didn't deliver what they needed. We put a stop to that, but in the process we examined what the end goals were for these projects and adopted their business requirements so that the new, consolidated program plan could accommodate the business. This helped us to get the business owners involved in what we were doing, which was distinctly lacking previously."

Charlie paused to ensure everyone was following and took a quick sip of water to keep his slightly constricted throat from going dry as he spoke.

"Because of the processes our team put in place, and you can credit Marc Miller and Jim Taylor with much of it, we've made massive improvements in our ability to gather requirements, deal with risks and problems, deliver software on time, interact with and train the user community, and remain aligned with what's happening in the various business units. The result of this is that the key architectural components will be delivered in line with the revised schedule, which we'll discuss in a minute. More importantly, the early returns on new product sales are ahead of projections."

Charlie was hoping for some smiles, or nods of assent, but received neither. Everyone in the room was interested. Some were scribbling notes and questions that everyone knew were to be held until then end of the presentation. No one showed any positive signs just yet. Charlie pulled up the next slide.

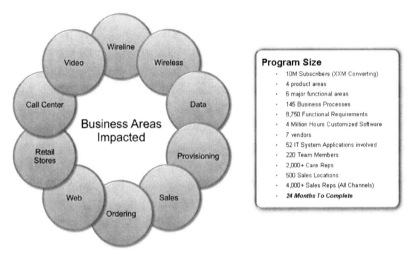

PROGRAM SCOPE

"This," Charlie explained, "is an overview of this program's massive scope. It impacts nearly every business area in the entire company. It touches all of our customers and impacts thousands of employees. We're talking about millions of hours of software-related work that will be required to complete it, on top of the work that's already been done. You can review these numbers at your leisure, but consider the 'in for a penny, in for a pound' nature of a program like this."

Eyebrows raised around the room at this last comment. He had everyone's direct attention, for better or worse.

"We're taking many measures to control costs, stay ahead of the risks, and ensure a smooth transition to our new systems and business processes. What we're doing though is like changing the trucks on a freight train while it's speeding across country. Even if you wanted to stop the train, it's not something that's done easily without derailing it and creating much bigger problems for yourself."

A few heads nodded. A few people stifled chuckles in their throats and covered them up with abrupt 'ahems.' Charlie wasn't sure if he was making the sale, but it seemed like most of the key folks in the room understood his point. He locked gaze with Liz Fagan for a brief moment and her glance said, "Keep moving." He clicked to the next slide.

Benefits Realization (2)

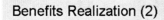

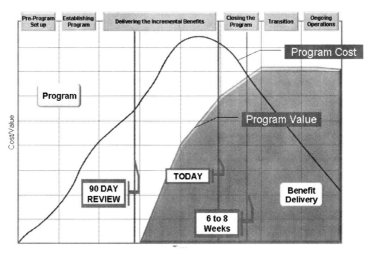

BENEFITS REALIZATION (2)

"I have to give Marc Miller and Jim Taylor credit for this slide. I think it does an excellent job of showing us where we were, where we've been since we met about nine months ago, where we are now, and where we can expect to be in the immediate future."

The Board members had seen a similar slide at the 90 day meeting and did not display the same confusion that they had at that time.

"In the first 90 days, we conducted a rapid discovery phase, instituted our program management strategy, revised the architecture and began shedding cost pretty quickly," Charlie explained. "We were able to accelerate the time to benefit on the core projects. But where you see those changes in the slope of the cost curve – first shallower, and then a bit steeper – that's where we clamped down on the budget, pulled back the scope, but subsequently invested in accelerating the program in a more efficient way. We had an increase in cost – which I like to look at as an investment – but we created a dramatic increase in the benefits we could derive from our activities."

Charlie paused for a moment to scan the room and ensure everyone was following him. He hadn't lost anyone yet, and if anyone was lost, they weren't going to let on among this particular group of people.

"There are a few ways we calculate the value of the program's results. One of the results of our program management approach is that it allows us to collect the information we need and actually measure different sort of benefits. What you're seeing here is the aggregation of cost reduction, revenue generation, decreased customer churn, and net subscriber additions rather than losses."

Roger Schultz raised a hand and spoke before Charlie could continue.

"How do you justify that benefits curve? It's awfully steep Charlie."

"Once we put our PMO in place and could see what was happening in the program, we were able to go after a lot of low hanging fruit. We cut out a lot unnecessary projects, consolidated some other rogue IT efforts under our structure, put tighter controls around the budget, and cut a lot of extraneous contractors. That's what I meant when I said we stopped the bleeding."

Schultz nodded for Charlie to continue.

"We were still increasing costs, however, because we had to spend to bring in the new architectural components that hadn't even been delivered. As we delivered those new systems, we began to derive benefits from them immediately."

The question that lingered in the air and Charlie could tell everyone wanted to ask, was "how do we get to the other side of the cost curve?"

"You can see that we hit the peak of the cost curve in the past few months. That's because we've run parallel infrastructure during the transition to the new platforms. In the past month, as we've brought the new systems and processes online we've been able to decommission some old systems and processes and bring that cost curve back down. We've also been able to reduce expenses because the lion's share of the development and integration work is complete."

Charlie paused again for acknowledgement before proceeding. He took a deep breath, stood at the head of the large oval table and put both hands on its lacquered surface. He looked around from face to face.

"Nine months ago my plan was to walk into this room today with a slide that only had two marker lines on it. That line marked as six to eight weeks – that's where I'd intended to be today. Now, experience told me that issues would arise along the way. I should have realized early on that this hole went a bit deeper than any of us even realized. But I was optimistic, maybe even hubristic, in my initial assessment."

The tension in the air was so thick that a filet knife could have sliced it. Charlie was gambling. In a sense he was undermining his own pitch. But he was betting that in this room, at this moment, being completely candid would earn him respect. He wasn't sure if he was right, but no one seemed to bristle at his words. They were taken for what they were - the plain truth.

"Now for some good news," Charlie resumed, breaking the tension. "I'm going to overshoot this time around and suggest that we are six to eight weeks away from the inflection point. We're on the downhill slope of the cost curve and are realizing increasing benefits in terms of reduced costs, improved operations, and revenue growth. Marc and Jim wanted me to say that we're more like three or four weeks from that point. I won't make the same mistake twice, even if I suspect they're correct because we have much better visibility into what's happening than we did nine months ago."

Brows wrinkled at this statement, but he had his audience bought into what he was saying. That was about the best he could expect after playing the mea culpa card.

"The best evidence we have is that we've launched our new web channels, online offerings, and bundle promotions in three test markets, and have launched pre-promotions in three others. At this point, our uptake numbers and revenue are exceeding the projections that backed up our business case. If that continues, you'll see that plateau on the benefits curve rise up more and we'll have hit some home runs as a result of all of this."

This time, Charlie didn't pause for reaction. He advanced to his next slide and kept talking.

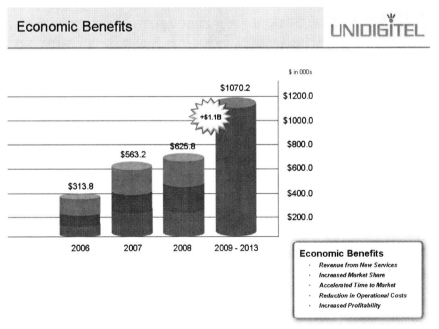

ECONOMIC BENEFITS

"What we're looking at here are our initial revenue projections for these new services. When I say initial I mean that if you drilled into these long term projections, we're ahead of this curve based on the early returns. Obviously the major economic benefit from a top line perspective is our ability to launch new services and keep new offerings coming to market faster for less cost. We're also able to bundle, cross-promote, discount, and bring cross-domain services to market faster than our competitors. Our marketing folks feel that's the edge we need to regain market share."

A few brows wrinkled and fingers were raised in lieu of hands at the term "cross domain."

"I'm talking about what you might have heard called 'three screens' types of services like programming your DVR from your cell phone, getting caller ID on your TV, or sharing content across your PC, DVR, and handheld. These are considered sticky services, and we think we can not only win more customers with them, but keep them in the fold."

Heads nodded, people around the table murmured with each other about the possibilities and Charlie let the chit-chat carry on for nearly a minute before continuing.

"What's most exciting is the bottom line benefit. The cost we take out of the business as we press on with the migration and legacy decommissioning lets us build our profit margin on all of these offerings, which also gives us some padding if we end up in a price war. Now, we want to avoid that, but it's nice to know that if a competitor tries to undercut us, we could theoretically sustain profitability at a price point that's in the red for them. We have some work to do to get there, but that's one of the major benefits of following through on our roadmap."

"On that note," he clicked his mouse, "this next slide gives you a high level view of our roadmap. I won't spend too much time here. I'm happy to answer questions about this at the end or offline. We've completed just about everything on this slide. We've done it effectively because of our governance structure. We ensure that scope doesn't creep; the budget is constantly clamped down; that we're considering the impacts on people, process, and technology – not just technology alone, but how it impacts the business and people in it. We communicate any

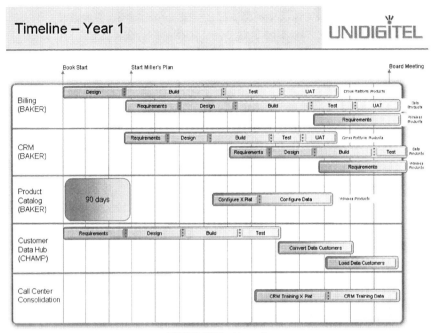

TIMELINE – Year 1

changes to the roadmap to you and our executives in real business terms. We're always asking 'is what we want to add or change aligned with the business goals.' If the answer isn't an absolute 'yes,' we don't do it."

If the members of the Board didn't already know that Charlie's approach to everything was a massive departure from Forrester's, they knew it now. Charlie was all business and gave the Board members confidence that even if he was slightly behind the schedule he'd hoped to meet it wasn't for lack of keeping the requirements and deliverables focused. Charlie advanced to the next slide.

NuView Program Update

UNIDIGITEL

Still have multiple systems but, plans to migrate
- X-Product on new CRM platform
- User acceptance is high. They like the new system

Order Products Customer Usage

Consumer CRM Commapps

Billing Engine Commapps

- New billing engine operational for X-Product
- New contract with vendor holds them accountable for meeting specific performance criteria to get paid

- Despite best effort data matching could not be completely resolved
- Recommendation that data be converted anyway and problems fixed in the new system

- New Web UI for ordering and service of new X-Product offerings is working well

Customer Data Hub Master-Dat

Customer

Customer

Customer

Customer

NuView Program Update

"As you already know," Charlie explained, "we radically changed our approach to the architecture behind this program. The best piece my predecessor chose was in his billing partner. We moved the product catalog and CRM projects into their footprint," the pointer outlined the box containing the billing, CRM, and customer components," to reduce customization and integration."

"Sticking with this billing platform allowed us to get billing for our new bundles and cross-network services into production on schedule. We added strict delivery criteria to Commapps' contract and have ongoing criteria that dictate the kind of performance, particularly in terms of billing cycle time and accuracy, they need to meet in order to trigger their payments." Heads nodded around the room.

Turning back to the people at the table, Charlie continued. "Eliminating the original CRM product set us back initially, but it cut a lot of long term cost and effort out of the picture. We're evolving the CRM functionality so we're focusing our implementation and the first stages of our upcoming legacy migration on consumer products. That will give us more time to work out some of the more sophisticated requirements and use cases we'll need on the business services side next year."

He outlined the customer data hub with his pointer.

"This area is the culprit behind our delays. Our customer data has such severe quality problems and is so disparate from system to system that the effort to match and consolidate the records is greater than we anticipated at first. We're using some offshore partners who specialize in this kind of hands-on work to catch up."' This point elicited some concerned looks.

"In the meantime, we're pushing forward with the customer data hub and have an effort to match customer data in the new platform. For a period of time we may have some duplicate customer records in the new repository, but they will be accessible to our upstream systems from one place."

Charlie flipped his slide again, noticing some shuffling among the participants. He knew the idea of pushing the customer data hub forward with what could be 'bad data' wouldn't sit well with those in the room who had experience with major data integration programs in the past, but he knew his next slide would change their focus quickly. He clicked his mouse.

"Now, to put things in perspective, here's where we were when we started."

Eyes widened around the table. The Board had seen this slide before, but it had far more impact when put into the current context.

"You can see we've made enormous progress. When we began, we had many more moving parts, most of which had problems. Because of all of these pieces, the initial test runs on the billing system were horrendous. The user community was unhappy, the web effort was off the rails, the product catalog component was no good, and the data wasn't clean. As I mentioned, it was an even bigger mess than even the folks working with it had realized."

Previous Program Issues

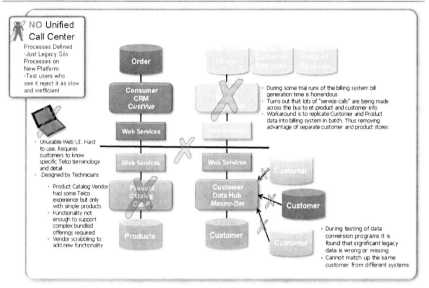

PREVIOUS PROGRAM ISSUES

NuView Program Vision

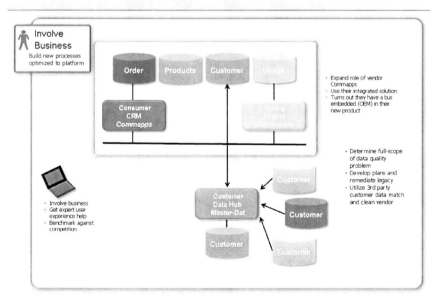

NuView PROGRAM VISION

"So those are just some of the reasons we scaled things back to this model. What makes me happy about this architecture is that this is the picture we showed you at the 90 day review. And if you compare it to the current state…let me just flip back for a moment," he did, "they are virtually identical, which means we controlled the scope very well." He flipped back to the Revised Architecture Plan slide.

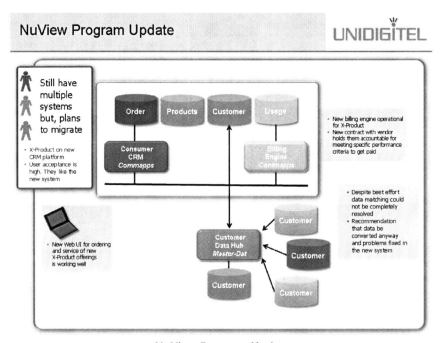

NuView Program Update

"In terms of the delta between the old and new approaches, you can see that we managed to eliminate the product catalog, because it didn't give us any advantages. Commapp's catalog was more than sufficient. It improved performance and cut down on integration and development time and expense. We eliminated the third-party bus for many of the same reasons and again went with what's built into the billing platform."

Charlie noticed some unasked questions from the group. He knew most of the folks in the room read the trades regularly, so he had anticipated their next question.

"So, let me just address these integration strategy changes. From a pure technology perspective, the new ESB is not as sophisticated as the old. But from a business perspective, it gives us what we need for far less cost and effort. The web services effort was put on the back burner as something we want to look at for late in year two or year three, once the heavy lifting on this transformation is completed. My predecessor's approach wasn't business driven and it was expensive. So, we've stalled it so we can build a better business case for it down the road."

Point taken. He'd said it earlier. If a project wasn't aligned with the overall goals – and wasn't absolutely necessary – it wasn't going to fly. Charlie wasn't funding Forrester's old skunk works. That was the bottom line. This was one of the reasons he and Lang Willis understood each other.

"Moving on, I mentioned the CRM change and you understand the issues there," Charlie scanned the room and received the nods he was looking for. "So the other point to take away is that we involve the business actively in what we're doing. That's why we have a successful web revamp happening and why the user community is happy with us. We're giving them what they want and we didn't force anything on them. We've included them at every step. Where my predecessor thought he'd accelerate things by going his own way, I can tell you first hand that the opposite is and has proven to be true."

At this point, Liz Fagan flashed Charlie a quick signal with her hand that said it was time for a little break. He nodded and said, "okay, I want to thank you all for your patience. Why don't we take about a 10 minute, uh, health break. When we come back, we'll talk about next steps and wrap up."

As several members of the Board filed out and headed to the washroom, Roger Schultz, Chairman of the Board, lingered behind for a word with Charlie. Liz Fagan had intended to give Charlie a few quick words of encouragement, but instead approached the two quietly. She didn't want to interrupt whatever but wasn't about to leave her sometime mentor to this wolf. Schultz extended a hand to Charlie.

As he shook Charlie's hand he said, "I'm not a forgiving guy Charlie and I'm not easy. But I'm not unreasonable either. You've done a lot for us and I appreciate that you're forthright about where you feel you've fallen short," Schultz said as he looked Charlie in the eye with his intense and unwavering gaze.

"I appreciate that Roger. I think it's largely because of the folks on my team who've really pulled this all together. I hope I can pass the positive words on to them after this," Charlie replied.

"You can bag the modesty act with me Dowd. You've done a solid job here, and I know you've been in the trenches with these guys. Let's call it a B-plus," Schultz said. Charlie wasn't sure if he was kidding him at all or not. He knew, however, that B-plus meant his head wasn't on the chopping block.

"That's fair," he said.

"Now I think we need to ask, 'what's next?'" This economy is a nightmare. The market is pounding us pretty hard. I see reasons why we need to push forward, but I'm going to need to understand more about the risks and the upside before we make a final decision," Schultz told him candidly.

"Well Roger, I think you'll see as we wrap up that the groundwork's been laid. But, maybe it will make sense for you and I, and probably Liz and Lang, to get together on this and finalize some of the big decisions we need to make coming out of this meeting."

Schultz hadn't expected this, but he was no stranger to rolling up his sleeves either. "Alright Dowd, I'll take you up on that. Let me see what you have to say today. But assuming it makes sense, we'll meet up next week at my club and see where we go from there."

"Funny," Charlie said, "I was going to have you join us at the diner. That's where most of the big thinking on this thing has happened."

Schultz cracked the slightest hint of a grin and said, "I can't stand the coffee in that place," shook Charlie's hand again while gripping his shoulder, and walked toward the door.

"That was encouraging," Liz told Charlie. "I wasn't sure for a minute what was going to happen there."

"Neither was I," Charlie said. "But you know, for his reputation and the whole cold-blooded routine, Roger's not a bad guy. I don't think I'd want him for a father-in-law, but for a Chairman he's alright."

"Yeah, he's not bad for someone who has to play it close to the vest," Liz said. "Anyway, I think they're coming back in. Did you need to step out first?"

"No, I'm good. I'm ready to get this over with."

Liz smiled and walked back to her seat as the other members of the Board resumed their places around the elongated table. Charlie pulled up his next slide and waited for everyone to get situated.

Program Risks and Issues

Economic Concerns
- Recession Economy
- Impact on Speed of Growth
- Reduced Access to Capital
- Declining Share Price
- Stability of Some Suppliers

Program Issues
- Continued Investment Necessary to Achieve Long Term Goals
- 6-8 Weeks Away from Inflection Point Where Benefits Surpass Costs
- Headcount has been reduced; Can't afford to lose key talent
- Year 2 and 3 Legacy Migration Could Reveal Some Added Cost and Risk

PROGRAM RISKS AND ISSUES

"If everyone's ready to resume," Charlie began, "I'd like to jump into some of the concerns moving forward and talk a bit about what happens next."

Nearly everyone nodded and those who'd been doing so prepared to take more notes.

"It's no secret that we might be facing some budget constraints given the economy's changing nature. I think it's wise to assume that, despite how positive the early returns are on our new services, there could be an impact ultimately on how fast we can grow, especially once we captured most of the low hanging fruit we're grabbing now. We can beat out our competitors for market share, but we might expect the overall spend per customer to back off a bit in the coming year if the economy stalls."

This seemed a reasonable conclusion to everyone seated around the table. Miller, standing at the back of the room, cringed a bit at this admission, which he felt might undermine Charlie's overall pitch. But Miller also knew the boss knew what he was doing.

"One of my direct concerns, in the CIO seat, is making sure that our suppliers are stable in the near future. One of the benefits of our new architecture is that it eliminates several suppliers based on pure risk assessments. We're left with players that we don't believe are going anywhere. That said, we'll continue to make these evaluations and we have detailed contingency plans in place should any of them ever falter."

"If I may," Lang Willis interjected. Charlie extended a flourish of the hand to signal him to continue. "We have managed to secure access to what I'd call sufficient credit from several of our banking partners, and we have a cash reserve we've managed to build over the course of the past year just based on some of the cut backs we've made. The share price is an obvious issue, but from a cash perspective, I'll reiterate that we're more stable than we might have expected let's say 18 months ago. So, excuse me, go ahead Charlie."

"No, thank you Lang. Turning back to the program, if we want to achieve the benefits we intend, we're going to need to continue to invest. If you recall, we're about 6 to 8 weeks from that inflection point where benefit starts to outweigh cost. We're on the downside of the cost curve, but those dynamics can change quickly if we make radical cuts in the budget today."

"As Lang inferred, we've reduced headcount across IT, especially in terms of contractors that were working on the projects and shadow programs we've either eliminated or brought under our PMO structure. But my concern is that if we make major cuts, especially pre-emptive cuts, we could scare off some of our best talent. We can keep reducing cost as we complete development and testing, but accelerating that process can have negative effects on our deadlines and on morale."

There was the slightest hint of a collective shrug regarding this last point, but Charlie felt it important to make sure these folks, who spent much of their time in the ivory tower, understood that people were what made this program work. He had a lot of time invested in bringing people back to a positive frame of mind. This point did not seem to be lost on Roger Schultz, however, who nodded subtly in Charlie's direction.

"We have some concerns that our migration and consolidation plans could reveal some added risks, similar to what we've seen already with our customer data. We're looking closely at these things and have accounted for them in our current, revised budget. But we know these are the major risks we need to stay on top of at each step we take." He clicked for his next slide.

Timeline – Two Year and Beyond

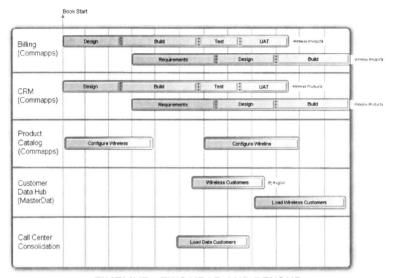

TIMELINE – TWO YEAR AND BEYOND

"This timeline shows our plans for the next two years. Much of the work, as you can see, doesn't involve new development or integration. Most of it involves legacy product and process migration, simplification, and improvement so we can leverage the new architecture.

The big question from here," Charlie clicked for his next slide, "is what happens if we throttle this thing back too far? I think the answer is that we automatically end up in the red part of this donut you see."

IT Projects –
Size and Complexity Enhances Risk

- Only One out of Every Ten Projects are Considered to be Successful
- Effective and Detailed Program Management is the Key is Success

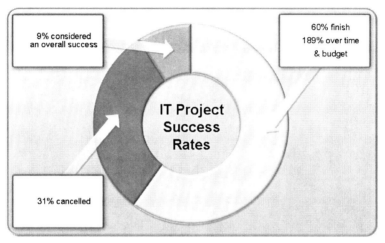

IT Projects – Size and Complexity Enhances Risk

"We want to be in the green, and we're on schedule to make it based on our structure, our governance, our engagement with the business owners, and our oversight by Mr. Willis' organization. The 60 percent of programs that finish over time and budget generally do so because they lack strong governance and let big problems fester. We're not making those mistakes." He clicked for his next slide.

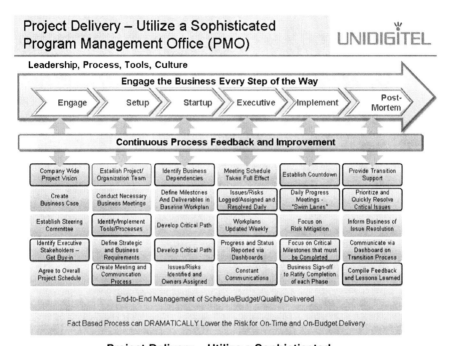

Project Delivery – Utilize a Sophisticated...

"I realize this is a complicated picture, but this is the proven model we use for managing this big NuView program. What you need to understand is that the nine percent of projects that finish in the green are the ones that combine this structure and these processes with the business aligned governance we discussed and the benefits realization approach we looked at earlier. The reason you bought me here is because I've done this before. The reason I brought Marc Miller in is because he's done this with me before. If we pull the plug now, you'll ensure that we've only built redundancy and cost into the business and we'll derail the new direction our business owners have set. If we press forward, I believe we'll be the market leader again and have an infrastructure and business flexibility that will keep us ahead of our competition for the next decade or more. The rest, as they say, is up to you."

Dos and Don'ts for Chapter 10	
DO:	**DON'T:**
Communicate the "so what" simply and clearly succinctly.	Hide or obfuscate problems and undermine your credibility. Don't be afraid to address real problems directly.
Keep your message to the Board simple.	Talk about effort, projects, deadlines, and technology without answering, "so what?"
Know your numbers - ROI, costs, etc.	Lose or try to confuse the Board with overly technical material.
Explain the results and benefits of your efforts.	Forget to present both short and long term benefits from cost and revenue perspectives.
	Avoid the hard questions or hide the real problems.

For more information on how EMC Consulting can assist you with your transformation visit: - **www.emc.com/services**

RECOMMENDED READING

Achieving Business Value From Technology: A Practical Guide for Today's Executive
Tony Murphy
Wiley
2002

The Balanced Scorecard
Translating Strategy into Action
Robert S. Kaplan and David P. Norton
Harvard Business School Press
1996

The Black Book of Outsourcing
Douglas Brown and Scott Wilson
Wiley
2005 (Updated 2008)

CIO Leadership Strategies: Impacting the Bottom Line as a Chief Information Officer (Inside the Minds)
"Ensuring Value For Wireless Technology Investments"
Dick LeFave, Vice President and Chief Information Officer, Nextel Communications
Aspatore Books
2005

Corporate Information Strategy and Management: Text and Cases
Lynda M. Applegate, Robert D. Austin, and F. Warren McFarlan
McGraw Hill Higher Education
2006

Customer-Driven IT: How Users Are Shaping Technology Industry Growth
David Moschella
Harvard Business School Press
2003

Delivering Superior Service
Electronic Data Systems Corporation
René J. Aerdts, Andreas G. Bauer, and Max R. Speur
AuthorHouse
2006

Designing, Managing and Improving Operations
David M. Upton
Prentice Hall
1998

Does IT Matter? Information Technology and the Corrosion of Competitive Advantage
Nicholas G. Carr
Harvard Business School Press
2004

General Management: Processes and Action
David A. Garvin
McGraw-Hill/Irwin
2001

Harvard Business Review on the Business Value of IT
Harvard Business Review
Harvard Business School Press
1999

Implementing IT Governance: A Practical Guide to Best Practices in IT Management
Gad J. Selig and Jayne Wilkinson
Van Haren Publishing
2008

The Innovator's Solution
Clayton M. Christensen and Michael E. Raynor
Harvard Business School Press
2003

IT Governance: How Top Performers Manage IT Decision Rights for Superior Results
Peter Weill and Jeanne Ross
Harvard Business School Press
2004

Levers of Control: How Managers Use Innovative Control Systems to Drive Strategic Renewal
Robert Simons
Harvard Business School Press
1994

Managing IT as a Business: A Survival Guide for CEOs
Mark Lutchen
Wiley
2003

Shared Services: Adding Value to the Business Units
Donniel S. Schulman, Martin J. Harmer, John R. Dunleavy, and James S. Lusk
Wiley Publishing
1999

Sprint Nextel IT Leadership: Reconfiguring IT Resources for Results
2nd Place Winner for Information Management
2008 SIM's Paper Awards Competition
LeFave, Branch, Brown and Wixom
2008

The Strategy-Focused Organization: How Balanced Score-card Companies Thrive in the New Business Environment
Robert S. Kaplan and David P. Norton
Harvard Business School Press
2000

Technology Benchmarks for Success: Leading Executives on Establishing Best Practices, Improving Return on Investment, and Creating a Benchmarking Structure (Inside the Minds)
"Moving the IT Rock"
Dick LeFave, Chief Information Officer, Sprint Nextel Corporation
Aspatore Books
2006

The World is Flat: A Brief History of the Twenty-first Century
Thomas L. Friedman
Farrar, Strauss and Giroux
2006

LaVergne, TN USA
28 April 2010
180951LV00002B/2/P